Beltane at Aphelion

Beltane at Aphelion
Longer Poems

John Matthias

Swallow Press

Ohio University Press

Athens

Ohio University Press, Athens, Ohio 45701
99 98 97 96 95   5 4 3 2 1
Swallow Press/Ohio University Press books are printed on acid-free paper ∞

Library of Congress Cataloging-in-Publication Data

Matthias, John, 1941-
    Beltane at Aphelion : longer poems / John Matthias.
    p.   cm.
    ISBN 0-8040-0983-X
    I. Title.
    PS3563.A858B4   1995   95-1275
    811′.54—dc20   CIP

Beltane at Aphelion is made possible in part by support from the Institute for
Scholarship in the Liberal Arts, College of Arts and Letters, University of Notre
Dame. The author also acknowledges support from two Ingram Merrill Founda-
tion grants awarded during 1984–85 and 1990–91 which provided time to work
on many of these poems.

A note on the title

Aphelion: the point on an orbit farthest from the sun. *Beltane:* May Day, and the time to propitiate Bel, Baal, Balor, Belenus, Beli—names for the sun at its most powerful; also names for the god that was once a goddess. The long poem stays in orbit, but only just, and celebrates its May Day in the January of its flight. Never exorbitant, but always spinning toward aphelion. And always celebrating Beltane there.

Also by John Matthias

POETRY
Bucyrus 1970
Turns 1975
Crossing 1979
Bathory & Lermontov 1980
Northern Summer 1984
A Gathering of Ways 1991
Swimming at Midnight: Selected Shorter Poems 1995

TRANSLATIONS
Contemporary Swedish Poetry 1980
(with Göran Printz-Pahlson)
Jan Östergren: Rainmaker 1983
(with Göran Printz-Pahlson)
The Battle of Kosovo 1987
(with Vladeta Vucković)

EDITIONS
23 Modern British Poets 1971
Introducing David Jones 1980
David Jones: Man and Poet 1989
Selected Works of David Jones 1992

CRITICISM
Reading Old Friends 1992

Contents

Poem in Three Parts

For Peter Michelson

Part One

I

wes cled in
a black gown
w/ a blak hat
vpon his

his faice was

his noise lyk

lyk the bek of ane egle gret bournyng

of an egle gret bournyng his eyn / His handis
and leggis wer herry His handis with clawes
His feit lyk / Wes cled in
vpon his

      Agnes Sampson

Agnes Sampson recording, official, brief: he had on
a gown and a hat which were both black. *Thank You.*
Thank you very much.

Agnes Sampson
Agnes Sharp
Agnes Stratton
Agnes Sparke

      Agnes Browne

      Agnes Wobster

          (Aberdeen: 1597)

Gentlemen

Somtym he vold be
lyk a stirk
lyk a bukk
lyk a rae
lyk a deir
lyk a dowg

He vold hold wp his taill

Lo! We kiss his arce.

Thank you.
Thank you very much.

and stript her there

a thing like
udder of a ewe
that giveth suck
two teats behind
her armhole there
her privie parts
and there as well
a teat a finger-length
and hairy
and

Deliver me

They searched her body founde upon her cunt
a lump about the bigness of a nut and wett and
then they wrung it with their fingers there and
moisture came like lee . . .

II

(a lantern there

or candle-light
I couldn't tell
a light a
phosphorescence there

a presence
and

I danced

a sound of pleasant instruments
a violin and pipes
a tamborine
and singing there

around the great gray stone
and through the painted
gate obscured by fog
a semi-circle then
a circle formed
and Him astride
the first of us
inside

one by one inside that ring
he took

and markt them there

III

in the kirk yard / with her daughters adoring

his member

        exceiding great and long / no manis
memberis so great and long / is abler for us then
than ony man could bee / is heavie lyk a stone and
verie cold as yce

     and stript her there

a thing like
udder of a ewe
that giveth suck

    abdoman 2

fundament 3
shoulder 1
pudenda 4

and under the arm

From which
familiars there
were wont to
suckle her . . .

Gentlemen:

IV

Gentlemen that gentleman
disappears in the East
cultivates beautiful manners
beautiful women
Engraves a heavy silver ring

                    with cabalistic signs

             Pious and elegant ladies

                  there

      at the Alloway Kirk

(Father, confess me
for I am pretty and blonde.)

(Bagabi! Lamac! Samahac!
she didn't *say* she was twelve.
Didn't *say* she wanted to
cultivate beautiful manners.)

                Reappears at Abbotsford

      told of
lonely roads: the others
walking in silence: a
bleating voice calling

from forest and plain.
(From the tips of her toes
to the crown of her head she
bathed herself with oil.
Then he took her quickly in the nave.)

Boredom? mainly.
(white monastic walls—
daughters there immured
and mortified)
boredom, mainly
leaden ennui
languid dreary melancholy days.

        Current of an inclination

             imperceptible contagion

             vaporous insinuation

    there

Tetanic immobility

Rigidity at first

Convulsionary epidemic in the end.

       Love

is license / All
the women his
Everybody manic or possessed.
In cities of renunciation
flagellants make law:
ecstasy makes criminals of girls.
Charges! Guilty!
(Fili Redemptor . . .)

      harden (oh, cannot) his hardest heart

Charges easy:
horny gods in trees:

every carnal field
a carnal synagogue
in May.
  Kobal! Nibbas!
Chancellor Adramaleck!
Emissaries, dignataries: post.

  Gentlemen, when exorcism fails,
  Drive along the highway to the coast.

I drove along the highway to the coast. Under sixty all the while and looking sharp. I had memorized directions; I had memorized my lines. I knew exactly where to go and what I'd say. No pants. No bra. I felt myself to be sure. I recited like a bull and like a dog. There was fog in patches and I dimmed the lights. Suddenly a lantern there ahead. I parked by the side of the road and stared: rigid, scared. Always this initial inclination to refuse.

  Always inclination

  Always to refuse

 who said we shall (they did) assemble

 (actual contemporaries)

 shades.

The army told congressmen yesterday it has enough of a single nerve gas in its chemical biological warfare arsenal to kill the world's population many times over. But Russia, one lawmaker reported, may harbor an even more lethal capability in this little discussed and highly secret field. The substance is labeled by the army "G.B." and the world's population is estimated at around 3.4 billion. Rep. Robert L.F. Sikes, D.-Fla, said he thinks the U.S. is not doing enough in the field. Sikes said it is estimated the Russians have "seven to eight times" the capability of the United States. The U.S. has enough "G.B." to kill the world's estimated population about 30 times. Russia, on the other hand, has enough to kill the world's estimated population,

  say

  160 to 190 times.

Part Two

Pale and Black, unparfyt Whyte & Red, Pekoks
feathers (color gay) and Raynbow whych shall
overgoe the Spottyd Panther wyth the Lyon:

> Croys byll
> bloe
> as lede:

F   e.s. .   Rs & m.

A .   . E

f.m.   w.v.

W

m. .   m&m.

(Bird of Hermes
Goose of Hermogenes
Two-edged sword in the hand of the Cherub
     that guards the Tree of life,
          etc.)

o.g.—o.s.—q.
p.g.—p.s.—p.q.
s.s.—s.m.—s.s.
    *
    *

```
*
*
*
*
*
*
*
```

      Mix and treat in
      philosopher's egg

         (one the
         Ram)

one the ram one the ram one the ram two the
bull one the ram two the bull three the twins
one the ram one the ram four the crab and the
lion and the virgin and the scales one the ram
one the ram and the scorpion and the archer and
the goat and aquarius twelve the fish one the
ram one the ram one the ram

      one the ram
      one the ram
      ten the goat
      four the crab
      two the bull
      twelve the fish
      one the ram

Visit the inward
parts of the earth,
by rectifying thou
shalt find

      a picture of the sun
      a picture of the moon

      the keys
      perhaps
      of Basil Valentine

to whose major premise

we should reply.
to whose minor premise
we should reply.
to whom we must
respectfully submit.

    And Oedipus said
    to the Sphinx:

    for a square of
    the elements in
    essence is
    triangular

    The hemisphere's
    two lines are
    straight and
    curved.

II

not until they died
because they mortified
not because they mortified they died
not because they died they mortified
not until they mortified
because they died

not homicide nor matricide nor suicide
infanticide nor fratricide deride
liquified and mollified and nullified
and petrified and purified replied
prophesied and glorified and rarefied
sanctified and rectified implied
classified and clarified and certified
typified personified allied
dignified and amplified and edified
modified and notified supplied
testified and satisfied and gratified
unified and villified espied
terrified and horrified and falsified
putrefied and ossified defied

not because they died because they mortified
because they mortified
until they died

III

The Illuminated
Brotherhood of Avignon:
every last illuminated
brother lied. And
Paracelsus, Flamel, and
Agrippa lied.
Roger Bacon lied.
Albertus Magnus lied.

Gilles de Rais
anticipating death
he told the
truth.

IV

the hieroglyphic figure
a dragon bites his tail
an emerald table and
the elemental sprite
the greater magistry
the humid path
the lesser magistry
the mystical drama of good
the composition of astra
the polarity of their molecules
the elements to which it belongs
the banner of Harpocrates
scion you congeal from 8 & 10
enigma & acrostic
the colors of the king
ubiquity of the end
primitive and proximate
the igneous principle there
the matrix of its acts
the value is 192

little cohesion draws
convex mirrors concave screens
a tingling metalline spirit
448, 344
an organ with seven pipes and an altar
rings on their fingers
swords with silver hilts
fine gay gloves on their hands
256, 224
to lie upon the primal waters
darkness of the world
a year in hiding or an influential friend
to undertake no study
the salt remains in the ash
the death of a man
the death, indeed, of a metal
take corporeal form
hidden by life
the severed heads of crows
a saffron-colored candle in the sky

such harmony / and yet this muddy vesture of decay

Whether the Canons were ever intended to be sung whilst alchemical experiments were being carried out cannot be determined with any degree of certainty. The actual bearing of the words of the epigrams on such experiments is by no means clear, as in no case do they suggest invocation or incantation. It is also difficult to believe that singers possessing the necessary musical knowledge and experience could be found amongst the laboratory assistants of the time; it certainly would not be possible to find

such assistants today

matter, he said,
expresses mysterious sound

music coeval with speech

number
weight
& measure

chymic harps

V

    (Tripod over Flame) Doth not attempt to transmute
into gold but summon Thot o ibis-headed god o Mercury
(Tripod over Flame) Doth not attempt to transmute into
gold but summon Thot o ibis-
                        headed god o Mercury of
churning elements hermaphrodite (Tripod over Flame) Doth
not attempt to transmute into gold but summon Thot o
ibis-headed god o Mercury of churning elements
hermaphrodite and over hell in flask a
winged dragon call (Tripod over
Flame) Doth not attempt to
transmute into gold
but summon Thot o
ibis-headed
god
    o Mercury of churning elements hermaphrodite and
over hell in flask a winged dragon call doth not
attempt to transmute into gold (Tripod over Flame)
doth not attempt to transmute into gold is no vain
cauldron-cook or chemist but for Thot will sweat
        whole days and nights before that
           furnace until face explode in boils
              and running sores (Tripod over Flame)
                  doth not attempt to transmute into gold is
                      no vain cauldron-cook or chemist but for Thot
will sweat whole days and nights
before that furnace until face
explode in boils and running
sores his fingers burn in
coals & clay & filth to
summon Thot o ibis-headed
god o Mercury of churning
elements hermaphrodite
and over hell

in flask

a winged dragon

call

(which shall be a sign unto you)

VI

sublimation
amalgamation
calcination
     (ascension
     fixation)
rubification
albification
     (ceration)

coagulation
imbibation
incorporation
citrination
     (cementing)

fermentation
inollification
induration
     (ablution)
mortification
mortification
Thot

sublimation amalgamation calcination
rubification albification coagulation
imbibation incorporation citrination
fermentation inollification induration
mortification mortification mortification
THOT.
          pot tobreketh / al is go

        Hermes Trismegistos, where?

VII

Sing-bonga, angered
by the smoke, sent
crows. Later he slept
in the furnace.

Sing-anga, earlier
and far away, a
fetus found and
burned:
    "on that ash
        erect a temple, Yakut shaman."

Yang & Yin
Yin & Yang

For the smith
and his bride,
these coals.

VIII

could boil,
melt
  (ego in
   hand)
his world.

therefore feared
as agent
  ("public
  menace")

matter unre-
generate
mirrors
(crime).

Verbum dictum factum: god in
the vowels of the earth:

ascribe unto
these metals,
Hermes,
need.

IX

(otherwise
perceive the imperfection
understand

not to imperfection
even otherwise
command

dross & refuse &
decay

ascend
condense)

Philosophy, he held, was out of hand.

X

Whether C. was
        duped "per doctrinam"
Whether C. knew
        Shuchirch at all

        William de Brumley, 'chaplain lately
dwelling with the Prior of Harmandsworth'—
does he lie?

Whether C was a
victim or student . . .

                (hermaphroditic rebis
                there appeared.

                Probably not.)

Probably not.

later,
after

XI

The still-providing
world is not
enough: we add.

Ponder matter
where impatient
sleepers wait.

And Aphrodite
saw her soul
was stone.

And Nargajuna
dreamed that
he was glad.

save and except the area described
as follows:

> beginning at the southwest
> corner of the Atlantic Beach
> on the Atlantic Ocean (the
> southeast corner of the property
> known as the Hoffman Property)
> thence running westwardly with
> the Atlantic Ocean waters to
> a point on the ocean two miles
> from the beginning thence northwardly
> and parallel with the west line of
> the Atlantic Beach to the waters
> of Bogue Sound to the
> northwest corner of the Atlantic
> Beach thence with that line
> which is the east line of the
> Hoffman property to the beginning

Save and Except.
Save and Except these lands.
Preserve the Saltar Path.
Alice Hoffman not allowed on
the Saltar Path. Saltar Path
no property of Alice Hoffman.

> Kitty Hawk
> Albermale Sound
> Manteo
> Roanoke Island
> Hatteras
> Cape Hatteras
> Ocracoke Island
> Pamlico Sound
> Portsmouth Island
> Core Banks

Shackleford Banks
Bogue Banks

approached by sea how
long ago, Davy
John Willis?

Robert Sullivan writes,
circa 1943: "I'd rather go to court than to the theatre."
Thus Mrs. H., circa 1943.

Durham
Raleigh
Goldsboro
New Bern
Morehead City
Beaufort
Bogue Banks

"Beaufort"
"Bowfut"
"Beeoofud"
Bogue Banks

North Carolina for the North Carolinians; Bogue
Banks for the Bankers.

(1)   *Storm after storm:*
        we cannot any longer
        hold this course: storm
        after storm: Hatteras,
        Cape Hatteras, Shackleford
        Banks: storm after storm:
        food gone: water gone:
        men near mutiny: we
        cannot any longer
        hold this course:
        Hatteras, Cape Hatteras,
        Shackleford Banks . . .
                    OUTPOST OF ISOLATION
                    300 YEARS 300 YEARS
                    SQUATTERS ON N. CAROLINA
                    SANDBANK THREATEN VIOLENCE

(2)   Through groves of
        twisted yaupon trees
        to the beach . . . a morning
        and an evening haul . . .
        barefoot on the sand
        and singing, singing . . .
        Settlers driven out
        of Shackleford by
        drifting dunes, out
        of Diamond city . . .
        Gardens would not
        grow in the sand,
        cattle could not
        graze, so back (how
        many years, John Willis?)
        to the sea

                    OUTPOST OF ISOLATION
                    300 YEARS 300 YEARS
                    SQUATTERS ON N. CAROLINA
                    SANDBANK THREATEN VIOLENCE

(3)   Formal gardens, cultivated
        lawns, fountains, arbours,
        fancy foreign friends. Once
        she brought a harpsichord
        from France. Who's the law?
        Judge A. Flint. *He* lived a long
        time ago. And here we are off
        Morehead City Bridge.
        Shackleford was sold to the
        state, Bogue was sold to
        the army. Now we've got
        Fort Macon and a
        missile base . . .

        Did they murder the cooks? Hack
        the Butler up? Did they
        drink the blood of
        the maids?
                            solid world / measure incomplete

                        ends and beginnings
                        cannot be regarded
                        as fixed

beginning at the southwest
corner of the Atlantic Beach
on the Atlantic Ocean (the
southeast corner of the property
known as the Hoffman Property)
thence running westwardly with
the Atlantic Ocean waters to
a point on the ocean two miles
from the beginning thence northwardly
and parallel with the west line of
the Atlantic Beach to the waters
of Bogue Sound to the
northwest corner of the Atlantic
Beach thence with that line
which is the east line of the
Hoffman Property to the beginning

it is understood and agreed and made a part of this judgement that
neither of the parties hereto will interfere in any way with the
full exercise of the rights of the other as adjudicated in this
instrument and that each of said parties shall be entitled to
exercise their rights or privileges as the case may be without
interference on the part of the other . . .

Thus the Judge . . .
and under his
breath:
                              'In the
solid world
measurements
are incomplete.
Time has no
stopping, divisions
have no permanance
and ends and be-
ginnings have no
fixity. The man
of great wisdom
observes both
far and near,
not thinking of
what is large,
knowing that

measurements are
incomplete. He
is aware of both
fullness and
emptiness so that
he neither rejoices
at life nor thinks
of death as calamity
knowing that ends
and beginnings
cannot be
regarded
as fixed . . .

(save and except the area described
as follows)

beginning at the southwest
corner of the Atlantic Beach
on the Atlantic Ocean (the
southeast corner of the property
known as the Hoffman property)
men with torches knives and other
implements of butchery destruction
desecration did intent on violence
thence run westwardly with Ocean
waters to a point on Ocean sands
two miles from beginning and thence
northwardly and parallel with
West Line of Atlantic to the
waters of the Bogue and thence
with waters of the Bogue to
northwest corner of Atlantic
Beach and thence along that
line to the beginning and did
terrorize the titled lady
living there (said Mrs. H.) did
sack the land did burn the
mansion to the ground did
rape and ravish slaughter and
profane did catch the chauffeur
cut away his genitals did murder cooks
did hack the butler up did drink

the blood of pink Parisian maids . . .

BUT

This cause coming on to be heard and being
heard by the court and a jury, the court having
instructed the jury that there was
NO EVIDENCE
NO EVIDENCE

Across Bogue Sound
The Tar-Heels
Saw a Castle
Rise.

Fires there, and
each man with a
torch. Crazy through
the houses
scattered round
the backbone of
the bank. Crazy
up the island nob
and down the
Saltar Path through
underbrush and
over dunes and
under over-
hanging limbs

Across Bogue Sound
The Tar-Heels
Saw a Jungle
Blaze.

Did they murder the cooks? Hack
the Butler up? Did they
drink the blood of
the maids?

solid world / measure incomplete

ends and beginnings

cannot be regarded
as fixed

. . . whereas there is now pending
in the district court of the United States
an action entitled
United States against 735 acres of land
more or less

Davy John Willis
sits on the beach
and mends nets.

Remembers little.

His ancestors were
pirates.

       Mrs. H.
was afraid of him
and of coral snakes . . .

               and of the jungle
               and of the swamps
               and of mosquitoes . . .

     (dunes drift, the
     sand covers
     the crops . . .

               And you have been here?
               Three Hundred Years.
               And your people?
               Fish in the sea.

Bucyrus

For a Class of 1968

❚

"Don't do that," said Aunt Ooney.

"Don't do that," said Aunt Olley.

"Don't do that," said Aunt Oam.

Don't do what? asked the midnight darkness pierced by Olley's flashlight beam. *And why not do it?* asked Bucyrus, dead Bucyrus, uncle of drawn curtains and tar-papered windows. *And why not do it, Aunts?*

"Your law forbids," said Oam.

"And Baxter rests," Olley whispered. "He rests everlastingly."

"As dianetical truth reveals," added Ooney. "As truth reveals."

But don't do what? asked Bucyrus through the night again. *Tell me Aunts of shadows.*

"Thou shalt not copulate on the floor at midnight," they all sang. "Up Aben, Up Ada. Get up. Thou shalt do thy Anglo-Saxon Grammar."

Olley took Aben by the arm. He had jumped to his feet when the light first splashed on Ada's face. Olley took him to a corner of the room and hit him twice across his nakedness with a short green stick. Ooney helped Ada back into her clothes, disentangling them from Aben's and throwing what was his to Olley in the corner. Oam lit the candles and opened up the text.

"Aside from the broad division of stops and continuants, consonants are further classified as liquids and spirants. They are also characterized by the places where they are made. Thus we speak of . . ." and Oam gestured that Aben should recite.

"Labials, dentals, nasals, palatals, and velars," he said.

Oam motioned to Ada.

"By combining these elements we can define m as a voiced labial-nasal continuant, k as a voiceless palatal stop as in kin, or a voiceless velar stop as in cool."

"All right," said Oam, closing the text. "Just what did you two think you were doing? Did you really think you'd get away with it? Did you think we wouldn't hear? Bucyrus taught us how to sense a fracture in the pattern even in our sleep, even sleeping soundly and dreaming of a holy discipline."

"Set the pattern, said Bucyrus," Olley murmured.

"Set the pattern," said Aunts Oam and Ooney.

And then, and then?

"He locked the door," said Ooney, Olley, Oam.

Silence choked the room as Bucyrus, dead Bucyrus, shuffled through. *Fail me? Could you fail me? Oam, dearest Oam, first born of Becky's shame, what has happened here?*

Olley, pray for us, tell us of the everlasting rest. Ooney, comprehend us, show us reasons for our failure and re-direct our discipline that it might restore the fractured pattern. And Aben, Ada. Aben, Aben, Ada.

"But it's our birthday," Aben said. "It's after twelve and it's our birthday, mine and Ada's. We meant no harm. We were only happy. Lying in our room asleep, I heard Ada stir. I was restless too, once wakened by her restlessness, and we began to talk. I will take the blame, I'll take it all. It was I who changed the subject willfully from Anglo-Saxon Grammar. It's after twelve, I said. Ada, it's our birthday. Happy birthday, Ada. We're sixteen today, I said. Sixteen years ago good Bucyrus brought us to his house and left us with our Aunts. And Ada smiled. Ada smiled and I knew that she was happy. I saw, though dimly, vaguely in the darkness of the room, that she was beautiful."

"And so you fornicated foully."

"Ruining everything."

"Breaking the pattern."

"Aunts," said Oam. "Aben, Ada. We must set the table. Bring the candles and gather all the texts of devotion and meditation. Make it elegant. We will discipline the night away and sleep tomorrow peacefully, one day everlastingly, one day with a cessation of all motion, of all which hath the nature of a means, and implies the absence of an end. . . ."

Here, there was an insistent, violent knocking at the door.

II

"Olley, Ooney; Aben, Ada; listen to your Aunt. Listen to your Oam. Bucyrus read us Exodus. Bucyrus read where it says honor thy father and thy mother, where it means, if there be no father and no mother, that an Aben and an Ada are to honor Aunts provided them by their benefactor. Bucyrus read us Leviticus: Ye shall fear every man his mother and his father. Aben, fear your Aunts. Ada, fear your Aunts. Ooney, Olley: listen to a chapter of Bucyrus.

"I, historian, keeper of the secrets of our origin, soul confidante and eldest Aunt, will tell a sixteenth birthday story preparatory to divine, grammatical, dianetical meditation and analysis. Olley Aunt, recite."

"This rest containeth a perfect freedom from all the evils that accompanied us through our course, and which necessarily follow our absence from the chief good."

"So be it. And Ooney Aunt?"

"The Preclear often will require a therapy allowing him to rid himself of those repressions and frustrations which deny a full, rewarding meeting with his auditor. So take him to your room and give him pillows. Let him throw the pillows at a wall. Let him shake them, let him stomp on them. Give the pillows names, and have the Preclear throw them at a wall."

"Well said. And now together with Ada, Aben."

"Oblique cases of nouns and adjectives are used adverbially, and from these, as well as from prepositional phrases, have sprung more or less permanent adverbial forms. These are genetive adverbs, accusative adverbs, and dative adverbs, Aunts."

"Then on, Bucyrus. On. Bucyrus was a large and rather awkward man, and left his house at seven-thirty. He had a handsome head of gray hair and wore a blue, double-breasted suit with a maroon tie. He always left his house at seven-thirty on weekdays, and it took him just under twenty-five minutes to walk to work. He was a teller, Aunts. He was a teller, Aben, Ada. A teller at the Jones-McMillen Bank of Franklin County, and he always walked to work. He always passed the Bennet Bar and Grill on his way to the bank, and always nodded to its owner who knew the teller would take his evening meal inside. The large, rather awkward gray-hair man arrived at the Jones-McMillen Bank of Franklin County some seven minutes before he was to open his window for eight hours of banking, Aunts. His was window number eight. Aben. And there were eight windows in all, Ada. Windows one through seven were attended by women—two widows and five wives. Often, the large, rather awkward gray-haired man was teased by the seven women concerning his bachelorhood. He was fifty-five years old and a virgin. He was a virgin, Aunts."

"'Aren't you lonely all alone in that little house, Bucyrus?'"

"'You'll be lonelier and lonelier as years go by.'"

"'An old man needs a wife, that's sure, Bucyrus.'"

"'He needs a helper, a companion—someone to grow old with.'"

"At five o'clock, Bucyrus closed his window and left the Jones-McMillen Bank. He nodded to the widows and the wives. By five-fifteen, he had arrived at the Bennet Bar and Grill to be served his nightly ham and cabbage by Charlie Bennet's first night waitress.

"'Milly quit,' said Charlie. Her husband took another job and they've moved out of town. This is Rebecca.'"

"'Becky,' said the girl."

"'Hello there, Becky' said Bucyrus."

"'Hi there,' Becky said."

"And right away Bucyrus loved her," Ada said. "He loved her right away, didn't he, Aben? I'm just certain of it, Aben. Up there in our room I think about it often. I'll study for hours and hours, study and memorize until I simply can't do any more, and then I'll close my eyes and think of Becky and Bucyrus: How he must have loved her. Say he loved her, Aben."

"I can't say it, Ada. I don't know. I wish you hadn't said it. I wish you hadn't even thought it, because now I'm going to have to watch."

Already, Olley had tilted back Ada's chair and already Ooney had pinned her arms to her sides. Already, Oam had crammed the Borax in her mouth and slapped her twice. Then, they lifted Ada from her chair and helped her to the sink. She spat into the sink, gagged, but did not vomit.

"Have you anything obscene to say?" asked Oam of Aben.

Aben didn't say a word. Aben didn't speak, but groaning in the corners Bucyrus whispered *Raped. I was raped,* Bucyrus said. *Attend to Oam's tale. It's a sixteenth birthday tale for Aben and for Ada.*

And here, there was an insistent, violent knocking at the door.

"Remember whence thou art fallen, and repent, and do the first works, and be watchful, and strengthen the things which remain. . . ."

"Coordinate your mind, coordinate the analytical with the reactive and let them merge. Know that the engram contains all passing perceptions, and train yourself to be incapable of error. . . ."

"Realize that the middle vowel is generally syncopated after a long radical syllable, and that it is retained after a short radical syllable, though the case-ending u of the nominative and accusative plural will disappear in dissyllabic themes. . . ."

"Better," said Oam, preparing to go on. "That's better. And now no interruptions, please. And so, Aunts, Bucyrus had met Becky. Bucyrus had met Becky, Ada. Becky had met Bucyrus, Aben. Becky and Bucyrus had met at Bennet's Grill. But, for a time, there was no threat from Bennet's waitress. She would seem to have menaced neither Bucyrus, nor his job, nor his principles of organization. She was merely the girl who served his nightly ham and cabbage. She was only the girl for whom he left a quarter tip.

"Aunts, Bucyrus lived by his principles of organization. He lived by the principles which we have inherited and which we will pass on to you, Aben and Ada. Bucyrus believed in discipline and order. He taught that discipline and order comprehend a here and now, prepare a there and an after."

"Make a life of Baxter," Olley said.

"Make a life of Hubbard," said Aunt Ooney.

"And make a life of Anglo-Saxon Grammar," said Aben and Ada together.

"Exactly so," said Oam. "Exactly so. Bucyrus made a life of Baxter and of Hubbard, of theology and of dianetics, and passed it on. For you, Aben and Ada, he suggested Anglo-Saxon grammar, and we concurred.

"From the Jones-McMillen Bank, then, he went to dinner and was served by Becky. For Becky, he left a quarter tip, and then went home. Home . . . here . . . Our house. At home, Bucyrus had his texts."

"Baxter," said Olley, "was born at Rawton in the parish of High Ercall near Shrewsbury on November 12, 1615. From his father came the puritan inspiration to seek the signs of his election, and later, a desire to awaken the careless of this world to thought of that other realm, that other world to be attained by the saints, by the elect."

"And Bucyrus was certain of his election," continued Oam. "He was as certain as our Olley here is certain. And Aunts, he studied. He studied and he memorized. From Baxter, then, the discipline required to attain another, better life. And from Hubbard, Bucyrus found a way of facing this one."

"Close your eyes tightly sitting in a chair," said Ooney. "Then imagine yourself in two corners of the room. Then go to those two corners, both at once, and watch yourself. In this way, Hubbard taught Bucyrus dianetics. He taught Bucyrus how to disengage his mind from his body, and how to understand the nature of his being insofar as it existed in this world and at this time."

"And so," said Oam, "Bucyrus studied and he memorized. He carefully taught himself that the noise and the traffic outside the bank was of no consequence. He taught himself to disregard the remarks of wives and widows. He taught himself, convinced himself to will his happiness, to impose upon experience an order and a pattern removing him from all that would interfere with his becoming self-known and ready for the everlasting rest. Any discipline, he thought, would so. Anything to avoid the essential unrealities. To know a discipline is to know oneself, he thought. To know oneself is to prepare for Baxter's rest. And Baxter's rest is the end, the culmination, and the joy."

"A glimpse the saints behold, though but in a glass; which makes us capable of some poor, general, dark apprehensions of what we shall behold in Glory."

"Set the pattern, said Bucyrus," Olley murmured.

"Set the pattern," said Aunts Oam and Ooney.

"Make yourself a life of Anglo-Saxon Grammar."

Because, Bucyrus said from corners, *beyond the discipline there is only danger and disorder. If we work eight hours, well, what then? Eight hours still remain before we sleep, and how are we to occupy ourselves? What are we to do? If you talk to wives and widows, if you follow their advice, they would rape you with a Becky before morning. I oppose them with a birthday tale, told by Aunts, my daughters. Listen to the stillness in the air.*

"Aben," whispered Ada, unheard by Olley, Ooney, Oam. "Aben hold my hand."

Here, there was an insistent, violent knocking at the door.

IV

"Aunts," said Oam. "Nightly ham and cabbage, nightly quarter tips, nightly smiles from good Bucyrus made this Becky wonder. Lord, Bucyrus was a kindly man. But often, his gentle nature lent itself to misinterpretation. The widows and the wives, for instance. My, Bucyrus is well preserved at fifty-five, they said. A healthy man he is, they thought, both in mind and body. A happy man he is. It's surely a result of virtuous living, they agreed. It's a result of all that study, of that discipline, and of that daily walk to work. He's fit to marry someone half his age, he is. The widows sighed: Too old, too beaten down with work and marriage and death, they thought. The wives thought of their husbands, young and strong. Would they grow old with dignity and charm? Rebecca, Bennet's ham and cabbage girl, had just turned seventeen.

"Bucyrus ate his ham and cabbage, smiled his kindly, gentle smile, left a quarter tip, and Becky wondered. She was not a widow and she was not a wife. She was seventeen, and she wondered. Bucyrus was a handsome, healthy, virtuous man. He was a fifty-five-year-old-virgin scholar and efficient teller at the Jones-McMillen Bank. And he always walked to work."

Oam stopped her recitation to replace a flickering candle. After the flickering candle was snuffed and before the new candle was lighted, in the total darkness of an instant without shapes and shadows, Ada leaned to Aben and kissed him on the lips.

Bucyrus groaned in the corners, and Ooney heard.

"Will you make us spend the entire week in castigation and repentance?" Ooney asked, separating hands and interlocking fingers. "Must you profane even the meditation table?"

Aben dropped his arms to either side of his chair. Hands dangling, he stared blankly into the newly-lighted candle flame.

Ooney placed Ada's hand in Ada's lap, and then gently, for a moment, stroked her leg and inner thigh.

"Please don't, Aunt," said Ada. "Not with Aben here."

"There are certain conventions that one must allow and accept," said Ooney, "before dianetical therapy can become effective, slut!" She reached for Ada's breast and pinched her nipple hard. Ada winced, then wept, and Aben sat staring into the candle flame waiting for Olley's hand to imitate the motions of Ooney's, though not on Ada's thigh, but on his own.

Becky, said Bucyrus, *never understood. She misinterpreted everything I said and did. I only wanted ham and cabbage, never Becky. Charlie Bennet knew me, and surely, had he cared at all, he might have spoken with her and averted the confusion that was to follow. Charlie, friend and brother, why not tell your waitress of the order and the patterns that our conversations take? Eight hours are for sleeping, eights are for counting money out as best as can be done, an hour is for walking back and forth, an hour is for eating ham and cabbage, three hours are for Baxter, three for Hubbard, and in this way I'll be self-known and ready. Ready!—Ready not for Becky, though. Tell your Becky I'm not ready for her. I'm fifty-five and I'm self-known and disciplined. I'm fifty-five and I avoid essential unrealities. Wives and Widows and Waitresses are essential unrealities. I'll have no daughter-Aunts to nurse, by God! I'll need no Aben and no Ada to correct my blunderings. I will not blunder, Charlie! Tell her I'll only eat my ham and cabbage, smile, and leave a quarter tip. Tell your waitress who I am now, Charlie Bennet!*

"Ooney," said Oam. "What are you doing to Ada? What are you doing to Aben, Olley? What is everyone doing?"

"Light another candle and I'll tell you," Ada said.

And here, there was an insistent, violent knocking at the door.

V

"Some nights ago, exhausted from my study, I lay down in bed and thought of Becky and her happiness."

"The whore, the slut!" said Ooney.

"I thought of how she must have waited for Bucyrus every night, of how she must of hated working at the Grill. She must have been as numbed and deadened after hours of serving ham and cabbage as I am numbed and deadened after three hundred lines of Anglo-Saxon. How alike, I thought, are she and I. Could she have loved ham and cabbage any more than I love glossaries and lexicons? No, I thought, she couldn't have. But then, how ham and cabbage must have changed for her when she served them to Bucyrus. Ham and cabbage were, I'm sure, utterly transformed into the very means, the only means of communication with her lover."

"Lover!" said Olley, "Bucyrus who was raped, her lover?"

"And so, as ham and cabbage change, Anglo-Saxon grammar changed when Aben asked me for a difficult declension. I knew it, and I gave it to him, and he kissed me for the gift. That's when Ooney came with therapy, she said, to restore the worship of our discipline. Olley came with her, bringing Baxter's prayer books, and she took Aben from the room. Ooney asked me to recite some fifteen paradigms, which I did. Then she told me to relax and close my eyes and to imagine Aben's face in front of me. She told me I should spit in Aben's face, and when I refused, she spat in mine. She told me once again to spit in Aben's face and then I did. Ooney gave me two heavy texts to hold—a dictionary and a lexicon. I held them at arms' length, with weary arms, and she told me I should imagine Becky's face in front of me and spit in Becky's face. I didn't do it, but she didn't spit in mine this time. Instead, she took off all my clothes, and while with weary arms I held a lexicon and dictionary in the air as though my hands were nailed to a cross, she kissed me in three places: here and here and here. I wish Aben were allowed to kiss me there, but Aben, who told me so himself at midnight, had to kiss Aunt Olley while he recited grammar and while she repeated Baxter's prayers."

"Aunts," said Oam, lighting still another candle wick. "Aunts, dear sisters. Don't I satisfy you, darlings?"

Here, there was an insistent, violent knocking at the door.

VI

"Bucyrus," said Aunt Oam, "arrived at seven-fifty-five. He nodded to the widows and the wives, and opened window number eight of the Jones-McMillen bank. In the middle of the morning, Charlie Bennet's Becky walked into the bank and up to window number eight. Becky didn't say a word, she only gave an envelope to Bucyrus. Then she left. She left the Jones-McMillen Bank and window number eight. Bucyrus opened up the envelope and read the note: Dear Bucyrus, said the note. I am seventeen and I am pretty. I can fix you ham and cabbage in your house and then you won't have to come to Mr. Bennet's anymore. I will fix you ham and cabbage tonight at six. I'll be able to because I'm going to quit my job and work for you instead. I am only seventeen and I am very pretty. Becky.

"Bucyrus wondered what to do. He had no idea what it was that he should do, and so at five he nodded to the widows and the wives, locked up window number eight, and left the Jones-McMillen Bank. He walked by Charlie Bennet's Grill looking straight down at the sidewalk, and then went home. Once inside his house, he locked the door. But what he had intended to lock out, instead he had locked in: Charlie Bennet's Becky smiled from the kitchen where she was fixing ham and cabbage for Bucyrus."

Who let her in? Bucyrus said. *What was she doing in my house? God knows how Becky got into my house. Look at each other through the candles on the table, through the shadows that I cast, through the patterns and the order which turns each pane of glass into a mirror throwing back a meaning to oppose the inanity of essential unreality into which I tumbled. Look at each other through the candle flame and ask. Look at one another through the shadows: ask. Look now Aunts and Aben, Aunts and Ada. Look into the mirror or pattern. Ask: How did Becky get into my house?*

"Becky got into the house because Bucyrus loved her," Ada said. "Bucyrus let her in."

"Recite your text!" said Oam.

"Becky got into the house because Ada says Bucyrus loved her," Aben said. "Please don't hit me. Please don't punish her."

"Recite your text!" said Ooney and Olley.

"Becky got into the house because Bucyrus. . . ."

"Becky got into the house. . . ."

"Becky got into the house because. . . ."

Because she broke the bloody kitchen window open, said Bucyrus. *She broke the bloody kitchen window open and started making ham and cabbage for my dinner. I only wanted ham and cabbage, never Becky. I wanted it at Charlie Bennet's Grill. Charlie Bennet's Grill, you see, is just half-way between my window number eight and my texts of discipline and meditation. Just half way, you see. I've always had my ham and cabbage down at Charlie Bennet's, never here. Here I've studied and I've memorized. I'll not have my dinner here with Becky, and I'll have no Becky with my dinner. But after it was over, after it was over, when what I didn't want to eat was eaten with Bennet's Becky with whom I didn't want to eat it, then she raped me. Raped me, raped me, raped me. Right in my own house among my books and on my kitchen table. Forgive me, Oam, daughter. Forgive me, Oam, Aunt. You were not wilfully conceived among those dirty dishes on that cabbage-covered table top.*

"Becky got into the house because Bucyrus loved her," Ada said. "Bucyrus let her in."

"Recite your text!" said Oam.

"Bucyrus loved her. Loved her loved her loved her."

"Recite your text!" said Ooney and Olley.

"Don't you stuff her mouth," said Aben. "Don't you touch her."

"I'll have some Anglo-Saxon or I'll have your balls," said Olley, picking up a knife.

"I'll bite your darling Ada's nipples off," said Ooney.

"We'll have some Anglo-Saxon grammar now!" said Oam. "We'll celebrate your birthday properly with birthday tales prescribed by good Bucyrus. We'll hear revolting histories of our conceptions and our births. We shall judge, condemn, and damn the Becky-slut, and damning her, we'll sing Bucyrus in the candle light and shadows. Rub my thighs and kiss my cheeks, my sisters. Read from Baxter and from Hubbard, Aunts. Give us Anglo-Saxon Grammar, foolish rebels. Come rub my thighs, come kiss my cheeks: Delight me."

"There are some verbs. . . ."

"There are some verbs which employ. . . ."

"Go on, go on!"

"There are some verbs which employ in the present exclusively forms of original ablaut preterites. Accordingly they are called preteritive present verbs."

On a cluttered table top, my life lost all its meaning. I had not eaten at my accustomed time. I had not eaten at my accustomed place. I did not read, or study, or memorize a thing that night. I was ravished all night long among the dirty dishes on the cabbage-covered table top where you were born.

"Aben," Ada whispered. "Say that you believe."

"Aben," Ada whispered. "Look at me and tell me you believe."

"Olley," Aben said aloud. "You can touch me if you like. You can touch me if you'll ask Aunt Oam to end the meditation. I'm very tired. I'd like to go to bed."

Here, there was an insistent, violent knocking at the door.

VII

"What an eternal Sabbatism then, when the work of Redemption, Sanctification, Preservation, Glorification are all finished and his work more perfect than ever, and very good indeed . . ."

"What a life without error when auditor and preclear at last connect in that final ever-revealing therapeutical climax which ushers in penultimate realities . . ."

"What strong declensions, used with case-endings which are of prenominal origin, which involve inevitably the masculine, neuter, dative, singular forms . . ."

"Excellent Olley. Exactly Ooney. But with more spirit, Aben. With more spirit, Ada. A birthday tale is being told, and you must be the chorus: sing loudly then. Sing the text and tune of good Bucyrus. Of good Bucyrus who in saintly charity provided you with what he lacked, with what he needed to insure continual perpetuation of a self-known state of grace through discipline: Aunts. Bucyrus had no Aunts, his daughters. No Aunts were present at that time to guard Bucyrus from all that clouds and falsifies. Had Aunts been present in the house Bucyrus built to wall off unreality and fortify his texts against the wife and widow which he swore all waitresses became, that initial rape of ham-and-cabbage origin had never taken place. We would have barred and bricked the window, turning Becky back to Charlie Bennet's Grill, back to Charlie Bennet's Grill half-way between the house Bucyrus built and window number eight, where waitresses might easily be wives and widows without fracturing a self-known ready life. We would have barred and bricked the windows, turning Becky back. We would have barred and bricked the windows, never to be born."

"Never to be born," said Ooney, stroking Ada's thigh.

"Had we been living," Olley said, "we would have seen to it that we were never born!"

"But we were. Born we were, the night of my conception. And I was first. Bucyrus tried to reason with her all the evening long. He carefully explained that if she quit her job then she would have no money. Becky said she needed none. Bucyrus told her that he made but little at the bank. She said that it would do. He showed her that he only had one chair, one table, and one bed, but Becky needed only stove, and sink, and cupboard. She wanted only to prepare a nightly ham-and-cabbage argument in opposition to a middle-aged virginity fortified by texts, expressed by morning walks, study by the light of candles, banking among the wives and widows, walks again by evening, dinner at the Bennet Grill, and sleep. Stove, sink, and cupboard were enough. Stove, sink, cupboard."

"And a disgusting, filthy table-top," said Olley. "How old are we, my sister?"

"I am forty-three, dear Aunt. Forty-three and several months. You are forty-two, and Ooney forty-one. We're growing old."

"The evening too is growing old. The birthday soon will pass and so the tale."

"Aben wants to go to bed. He wants to sleep so desperately that he is willing to concede and place your hand where you would place it."

"But Ada would deny Bucyrus, would deny the meaning of a birthday tale."

"Ada would deny."

And why, my orphaned youngest one? Why when Oam knows what happened from the first, explains it all so simply and so reasonably, must you insist that everything was otherwise. You, unborn, absent when what happened happened, uninstructed, uninformed by me regarding what I did and what was done to me, how can you reject the history recounted by our eldest Aunt, my daughter?

"And Ada would deny," repeated Olley.

"Deny she may, but she may not resist. So on until we write an end for our unwritten tale of Aben and of Ada, of Becky and Bucyrus. Of Bucyrus whose self-known ready life expired because a waitress broke into the house expropriating stove and sink and cupboard, whose stove and sink and cupboard once turned against their owner were the source of ham and cabbage different far from any one might find at Charlie Bennet's.

"And so Bucyrus died and we were born. Born of a rape which, repeated nightly on that table-top for some three years, resulted in first one Aunt, then two others. Becky never left the house, once, by error, she was that night initially locked in. Becky happily attended to the kitchen, attended to the stove and sink and cupboard, attended to the ham and cabbage, attended to the nightly rape. And while Bucyrus maintained appearances in dealing with the widows and the wives, while he seemed to be self-known and ready to all and any signing checks at window number eight, Charlie Bennet missed him at the Grill. Charlie Bennet thought it likely that his missing waitress was now engaged in serving meals exclusively to customer Bucyrus. He thought it likely that what had happened on the cabbage-covered table top had happened. And he thought it would continue."

And it did continue, said Bucyrus. Continued for three whole years until I had to steal from the bank in order to provide for you. Three daughters. What was I to do with daughters born of Becky's shame and of my violation? How was I to look into the faces asking me, asking me again and always asking me the nature of their origin with their origin such as it was? Oh, and it continued. To provide for you, I embezzled from the bank and walked by Charlie Bennet's not to stop for dinner or for conversation. To provide for you I embezzled and I walked by Bennet's Grill staring at the ground, walked by Bennet's Grill and walked on home to Becky. Home where Becky waited by the table of my dinner and your birth; home where faces asked me of their origin, where faces asked me of their future, asked me of my past; home where I resolved that the future of the faces was to be a mirror of my past, redeeming me and earning by their discipline my rest. Oh, and it continued.

"Oh, and it continued," Oam said. "Continued until the day Bucyrus walked out of the Bank with money enough to send the Becky-slut, the agent of our cursed birth, three thousand miles away with still another sister-Aunt inside her doomed to face a life companionless, sister-less, patternless, alone. He sent the Becky-slut away at last, and who would even dare suppose that Jones-McMillen money paid the fare? No one ever did suppose and no one dared suspect: but Bucyrus paid the fare with Jones-McMillen money."

"Taken, said Bucyrus, cautiously and cleverly. No one ever knew. I planned three years. I planned it from my very fall, planned the means whereby I might attain vicarious redemption. Becky, Becky. Far away I sent you: die then. Die. You came into my simple house unwanted, uninvited. You broke somehow into a kitchen window. There you were when I arrived. The pattern that you broke, the life that you destroyed, you destroyed and you broke with daughters. Call them Aunts. Call them Oam, Olley, Ooney: call them Aunts. I'll send you far away and uniformed with Jones-McMillen money. As a waitress you came in the window, as a waitress out you'll go. Out you'll go a waitress, or a widow if you will, and though I'll not again be ready and self-known, your daughters will. Our Aunts will learn the pattern of a discipline and teach it to their young. Our Aunts are women, and so they'll be, and that will be enough for them. They'll have their texts and they will have each other to examine. But against the broken pattern of Bucyrus I'll impose an Aben and an Ada who will make a life of Anglo-Saxon grammar. Taught by Aunts my daughters, they will make a life of discipline and memory that must necessarily redeem me. Everyone recite!

Here, there was an insistent, violent knocking at the door.

"And doubtless the Memory will not be idle, or useless, in this blessed work. If it be but by looking back, to help the soul to value its enjoyment . . ."

"The preclear from his corners reaches out to touch the Auditor between her legs. From his corners, from his meditation, from his cautious touch a pattern can be reestablished and a preclear can be free. . . ."

"Verbs with an originally short radical syllable, those which admit of gemmination of the . . . Help me, Ada. Help me say it."

"Recite your text!" said Olley, Ooney, Oam.

Sing together loudly for redemption, said Bucyrus.

"Verbs with an originally short radical syllable . . ."

"Ada."

"No. No no no no. I simply don't believe it."

Here, there was an insistent, violent knocking at the door.

VIII

Olley and Ooney had already reached for the Borax which they would stuff in Ada's mouth. Olley held the short green stick with which she intended to slash at Ada's cheek. Aben stared into the candle flame, waiting for the sound of slaps and gagging, but Oam spoke: "Tell us, Ada," she said, and kissed her breast. "Tell us what you don't believe."

"I don't believe a thing you've said. Not a single word."

"And just what is it you believe?" asked Olley.

"I believe Bucyrus was in love with Becky."

Never, said Bucyrus. *Never did I love. I was raped each night upon a cluttered table-top and ravished of my meaning and my aim.*

"I believe Bucyrus was in love," repeated Ada. "I don't believe a thing you've told me and I don't believe in Anglo-Saxon grammar."

"Then explain your life to me," said Oam. "What are you about? Where have you come from? What are you doing here? Where are you going?"

"I have no idea, Aunt. Can it matter."

"Can it matter?" said Aunt Oam. "Can it matter? Is it of no importance that Bucyrus, turning eighty, found you along with Aben in an alley, cold, alone, and hungry? Is it of no importance that as speechless children he brought you to his daughters, young and handsome then, for food and warmth and learning? Is it of no importance that he gave not only life, but a life of order and of meaning relating you to him through us, your Aunts? Is it of no importance that a birthday tale is being told informing you at last of what it means to live a life of discipline with Aunts by revealing links and parallels from a chapter of Bucyrus?"

"To me, it matters not at all, Aunt Oam. I don't believe that what you say is true. I think it otherwise."

Silly, foolish Ada, said Bucyrus. *Silly, foolish child. She repeats exactly what I told her on the night we set the pattern once again, on the night I left the house and locked the door and walked into the snow at eighty-three to die. She repeats exactly what I said and told her to repeat and sing to you this birthday night.*

Here, there was an insistent, violent knocking at the door.

"And what have you to say then, silent Aben?" Oam asked. "Are you hostile or indifferent to the revelation of your origins?"

"I am neither hostile nor indifferent. I'm only tired. It must be morning now, and I'd like so much to end the meditation and to go to sleep."

"Aben, you're afraid," said Ada. "You're very much afraid."

"It's true. I'm very much afraid."

Here, there was an insistent, violent knocking at the door.

"I believe," said Ada, "that if Bucyrus ever lived at all, Bucyrus was in love with Becky. Becky I believe in. Becky was alive. And if she broke into a house that was in any way like this one, then she did well. If Bucyrus only wanted me to memorize my Anglo-Saxon and to lie beside Aunt Ooney in the night while she nibbled at my body asking me to make secure the pattern, then Bucyrus never lived. If Bucyrus only wanted Aben to recite what he had learned, to repeat upon command the prayers of Baxter while Aunt Olley slipped her hands into his pants, then Bucyrus never lived. If Bucyrus wanted all of you—Ooney, Olley, Oam—to lie triangularly in your giant bed and whisper perfumed, scented secrets of Baxter and of Hubbard breathlessly between the spread and outstretched legs of one another, then Bucyrus never lived. But if all you've told me is a lie, if all you've done with us is an even greater lie, then perhaps Bucyrus lived. I believe that Becky lived and that

Becky walked into the house. And since I believe that Becky lived, then it seems to me Bucyrus lived as well and that he let her in the house through the door he opened. And since I do believe that Becky and Bucyrus loved, that Bucyrus let her in the house by opening a door, I don't believe a thing you've told me of my origin. I have no idea where I came from. Can it matter? I have no idea why I'm told to study and to memorize and to sleep beside Aunt Ooney. And I reject your explanation. And I believe that if Bucyrus lived, Bucyrus loved. And I love Aben. I love you, frightened coward!"

And here, there was an insistent, violent knocking at the door.

"What are you doing?" Aben said. "You aren't making sense. You're saying things that justify unending recitations at a meditation table burning candles through both night and day."

"I've said that I love you, Aben. And I've said I choose to believe that Bucyrus loved Becky who was alive."

"If Bucyrus loved her, then what's the meaning of these years we've lived here with our Aunts?"

"A lie. A hoax. I just don't care. It makes no difference what it means.

"Stuff the Borax in her mouth. Hit her with the stick."

"Get a grammar book, a lexicon . . ."

"Make her eat a passage from The Everlasting Rest . . ."

"I choose to imitate the life it seems to me that Becky led. I'm going to see who's at the door."

"Set the pattern, said Bucyrus."

"Make a life of Anglo-Saxon grammar."

"I choose to imitate the life it seems to me that Becky led."

"This rest containeth a perfect freedom from all the evils that accompanied us through our course, and which necessarily follow, which follow . . . which follow . . . which follow which follow. . . .

WHICH FOLLOW

which follow which follow which follow which follow which follow follow follow follow follow follow follow follow follow follow. . . .

I choose to imitate and see.

So take him to your room and give him pillows. Let him throw the pillows at a wall. Let him shake them, let him stomp on them . . . stomp . . . stomp. . . .

STOMP ON THEM

stomp on them stomp on them stomp on them stomp on them stomp on them stomp on them stomp on them stomp on them stomp on them stomp on them stomp on them stomp on them stomp on them stomp on them stomp on them. . . .

I choose to imitate the life.

Because, beyond the discipline there is only danger and disorder. If we work eight hours, well, what then? Eight hours still remain before we sleep, and how are we to occupy ourselves . . . occupy ourselves . . . occupy ourselves . . .

OCCUPY OURSELVES

occupy ourselves occupy ourselves occupy ourselves occupy ourselves occupy ourselves occupy ourselves occupy ourselves occupy ourselves occupy ourselves occupy ourselves. . . .

What are we to do?

Imitate the life.

Sing together loudly for redemption.

Verbs with an originally short radical syllable . . . Ada, help me. Ada, please. . . .

Imitate the life and see.

Aren't you lonely all alone in that little house, Bucyrus?

You'll be lonelier and lonelier as years go by.

An old man needs a wife, that's sure Bucyrus.

He needs a helper, a companion—someone to grow old with . . . grow old with . . . to grow old with. . . .

OLD WITH

old with old with old with old with old with old with old with old with old with old with old with old with old with old with old with old with old with old with. . . .

And so you fornicated foully.

Ruining everything.

Breaking the pattern.

Right in my own house among my books and on my kitchen table: Raped me raped me raped me raped me raped me. . . .

RAPED ME

raped me raped me raped me raped me raped me raped me raped me raped me raped me raped me rape me rape me rape me rape me rapeme rapeme rapeme rapemerapeme rapemerapeme rapemerapemerapeme rapeme rapemerapemerapemerapeme. . . .

We'll judge, condemn, and damn the Becky-slut.

We'll sing Bucyrus in the candle light and shadow.

We'll judge, condemn, and damn the Becky-slut.

We'll sing Bucyrus in the candle light and shadow.

SHADOW SHADOW

shadow shadow shadow shadow shadow shadow shadow shadow shadow

SHADOW SHADOW

We'll hear revolting histories. Conceptions and our births.

We'll hear revolting histories. Conceptions and our births.

We'll hear revolting histories. Conceptions and our births.

Come rub my thighs.

Come rub my thighs.

Come rub my thighs, come kiss my cheeks.

Come rub my thighs, come kiss my cheeks.

Come rub my thighs.

Come rub my thighs, come kiss my cheeks.

Come rub my thighs, Come rub my thighs. Come rub my thighs. Come rub my thighs and rub my thighs and rub my thighs and rub my thighs and rub my thighs and rub my

thighs and rub my thighs and rub my thighs and rub my thighs and rub my thighs and rub my thighs and rub my thighs and rub my thighs and rub my thighs and rub my thighs and rub my thighs and rub my thighs and rub my thighs and rub my thighs. . . .
COME KISS MY CHEEKS
THERE ARE SOME VERBS

The Stefan Batory Poems

for Cynouai and Laura

To begin with a name—
Katarsky—
                To begin
to leave with a name, Polish,
for a Polish ship named
for another, for Stefan Batory.
                Name of Katarsky.
Name of Stefan Batory.

To begin to leave this place
I've lived that's no more
mine than his, Katarsky's,
a village near his farm,
a land that's rich with legends
not my own, not his.

Name of Katarsky. Names
of his twins, Andrzej & Zbyszek.
Slid down haystacks with
my wife, these twins, when
she was five.
                Andrzej & Zbyszek.
Katarsky.
                After the war
when hay grew again
into haystacks, when the Poles
in England, some of them,
went home . . .

Katarsky, says the lady in
the shop Oh Well Katarsky sir
I'll tell you what I know
about Katarsky and that farm
and how he might as well have
gone on home the Russians *or*
the Germans and I
have to interrupt, say

no, oh stop it now
I only wanted
a Polish name for a poem:
only wanted a way to say goodbye.

Two

I wake up having dreamed of whales
To find my family sleeping in
Their berths. The breakfast menu
Is under the door: delicious
Smells in the pasageway . . .

I can have Soki, Zupy Sniadaniowe, Jajka, Omlety, Ryby, something from the Zimny
Bufet, Przetwory Owocowe on my bread, Sery, a hot cup of Kawa bez kofeiny (coffeinev-
rije: decaffeinated). Or mint tea and compôte. The day's program includes Holy Mass in
the Cinema, a matinée concert of chamber music (Vivaldi, Handel, and Telemann), after-
noon tea, an American film with dubbed-in Polish, cocktails, bingo and dancing. Wife nor
daughters stir. I open Mickiewicz. . . .

"Ye comrades of the Grand Dukes of Lithuania, trees of Bialowieza, Switez, Ponary,
and Kuszelewo! whose shade once fell upon the crowned heads of the dread Witenes and
the great Mindowe, and of Giedymin, when on the height of Ponary, by the huntsmen's
fire, he lay on a bear skin, listening to the song of the wise Lizdejko; and, lulled by the sight
of the Wilia and the murmur of the Wilejko, he dreamed of the iron wolf. . . ." What an
invocation! Comrades and trees! The trees are important.

Last night as we passed Land's End I spoke for hours with a couple from Newcastle
leaving England to emigrate to Canada. They stared hard, saying goodbye, looking into
the darkness for a last flickering English light. They're sorry to leave but can't, so they told
me, save a sixpence in a year. I wished them luck in Canada. And comrades. And trees.

I decide to go on deck.

Three

You, Batory, an *elected* monarch.
You owed it all to Henry de Valois.
Lithuania backed the Russian Tzar,
The Church took the Archduke; the
Anti-German *szlachta* was for any
Anti-German. You from Transylvania.
But leave it to the French:
Ambassadorially, the Bishop of
Valance distributes rings to
Get the throne for edgy de Valois.
Who took one look and fled:
Brother Charles croaked
And he (Valois) was Henry Three
Sipping port in Paris.
The horsy gentry blinked and summoned—
Married you to Royal Anne Jagiellon.

How much did you know? Not as much
As Canon Koppernigk who made
His measurements at Frauenburg (which
He called Gynopolis) pretending in
His *Revolutions* that he stargazed
On the Vistula away from battlefields
And Teutonic Knights. Not as much
As Koppernigk whose system, Prince,
Because he longed for Cracow
And his youth, would run your ship
If not your ship of state aground,
But this at least: How to maintain
Access to the sea; how to use
A chancellor's advice. And how
With Danzig yours to drive with
Peasant infantries the Russian Bear
Beyond Livonia to the Pope.

The cavalry was not deployed—
Horses in their stables, and at hay.

Four

A day passes, the weather is rough. We meet Poles, Englishmen, Irish, Americans, Czechs, Swiss, Frenchmen, Germans, Russians, and two Japanese. Diana teaches Laura how to approach a new friend: *Was ist Ihre Name, bitte? Was ist Ihre Name?* It turns out to be Alma. Laura is delighted. Cynouai is seasick and goes early to bed. It's my night for the movies.

The Cinema is down a flight of stairs outside the dining room—and *down, low,* so very low in the ship the room should be some kind of hold or place for ballast. In the middle of *Little Big Man,* I realize with a start that I am actually under water. If we spring a leak, this theatre will instantly fill like a tank, the watertight door will be closed by a panicky steward, and there we'll be—each of us holding his nose and floating to the ceiling as Dustin Hoffman shrieks in Polish and tomahawks fall from the sky. . . .

Was ist Ihre Name, bitte?

Was ist Ihre Name?

Five: The Library

I

The weather improves. Serious now,
I attend to correspondence.
Here they read the news and study
Not Mickiewicz or the other unread
Poets on these shelves
But ups and downs of stocks
And the extraordinary language
Of my President reported in the
Daily Polish/English mimeo gazette.
The banalities and rhetoric of power
Dovetail with the mathematics
Of the market: Soon the brokers,
As in 1929, will sail nicely
From the upper stories
Of the highest buildings in New York,
Their sons will pluck the feathers
From their hair and look for jobs
A thousand miles from the ethnic
Bonfires of their dreams, the
Poor will stand in bread lines,
And I, a curio from 1959, will find
My clientele reduced to nuns
And priestly neophytes. I return
To Indiana—the only place
Save Utah where the Sixties,
Though Peter Michelson was waiting,
Failed to arrive.

II

I am, as Peter thought I would be,
Going back. But slowly.
The journey takes nine days.
Unanswered letters—his and Ernie's,

Kevin's, Mrs. Harris's—
They weigh on me.
My friends, my gifted student,
My daughters' much beloved nurse.

"Too much mopin' now," says P.,
"And many mumblin's . . .
     But you *will*
Be coming back because although
You think yourself no gringo, John,
You are: and this is where
The gringo fighting is.
Or gringo baiting.
Or: whatever the conditions will allow.
I'll expect you here in August."

And Kevin writes: "I'm scared
Of everything and wholly lack
Direction . . .
     Plus, of course,
I'm personally responsible
For all of human misery: the
Shoeless Appalachians, every
Starving Indian. And what
I like to do is eat, talk to
Charming educated people, drink
Good wine, read the best
Pornography, discuss at leisure
Every new advance
In Western decadence."

E. has written to me once a year for eight years straight. This year it's about my poems. And his. His muse grows younger (he is over sixty-five) as mine begins to age. My attraction to quotation, commentary, pastiche: exhaustion? or the very method of abstention that he recommends? Many days I'd be a scribe, a monk—and I, like monk and scribe, am permitted to append the meanings that my authors may have missed. "He abandoned himself to the absolute sincerity of pastiche": on Ekelöf, Printz-Påhlson. Otherwise? Poets know too much. We bring things on us. There is always an extra place at the table: the poem, as Ernie says, arranges it . . .

With total serenity
He abandoned pastiche for patchouli
For patchouli and panache

He abandoned his panto-panjandrum
With utter contempt for panache
He abandoned patchouli
He abandoned himself with unspeakable simplicity
To Pastrami.

Inventions organized to dance
A variation of our lives?
Or simply evidence?
Or letters to and from our friends?
Here, the doctor said, is your scarab.
Prospero whispers in one ear
And Lenin in the other.

Six

Familiar, the dull rattle
and buzz of screws
abates; we glide. . . .

A hundred yards away
Gothic dips and spires—
St Brendan's "floating crystal castle."

Calving from some ancient
ice sheet, pinnacles around a central
mass like sails,

it makes good time: radar brought
back only sea return—echoes from the waves.
A spotlight caught it in the fog.

Late, late . . .
Are we in Brendan's time?
We suffer sea return.

The ship will tilt on its keel,
roll on the last wave
over the edge of the earth.

Seven

The Batory, a passenger says, once belonged to the Holland-American line; it was, indeed, the famous "Student Ship." If this is true, my strange sense of *déjà vu* is explained by more than the simple fact of my being, after sixteen years, at sea again. Can it be, in fact, that I am on the "Student Ship" once more? which flies the colors now of Poland?

Every detail has seemed so extraordinarily familiar: the location of rooms, the structure of the decks (did I kiss that girl from Georgia *there,* just *there?*), the clever organization of space which makes what is tight and constraining appear to be comfortable and larger than it is. The same ship! I was on my way, eventually, to Turkey, where I thought to save my small-town childhood love from becoming an adult. She had spent a year in Istanbul with her parents; her letters had grown sophisticated and knowing; I was afraid. Seventeen and virginal, I sailed from New York thinking I was Henry James and clutching to my heart every available illusion about myself and the world.

Ghosting on the bridge or in the engine room, hailing Flying Dutchmen or staring darkly at the sea, any foolish sentimental shade aboard is mine.

Eight

Two violins, a double-bass,
Drums, piano, and trumpet—
Accordion, of course:
A curious sound.
For our tea they play us schmaltz
And polkas.

At night, the same musicians
Are transformed: they make
A fearful frantic jazz-cum-rock
With other instruments
And sing a polyphonic polyglot
Appropriate to
Mid-Atlantic revels.

On a sleeve, four gold rings of lace, an anchor above; on another, three gold rings. I point out the captain and his second officer at an adjacent table. Cynouai: "Then who's driving the boat?" Laura: "It drives itself."

Over cakes, I polish my translation from the sixteenth century Polish of the famous Jewish Cossack, Konrad Konrad. He is not, unlike Michelson, Matthias and Sandeen, altogether serious in his treatment of the terrifying retribution falling upon the unfortunate bard as a reward for the practice of his craft. Thus I render the piece for a vanished upper-upper British accent and into an idiom which I think would not displease, say, Edward Lear.

Nine

Edgar Allan Poe
Wanted to go
To Poland.
So, probably, did Lafayette.
In 1830 he was too old.
James Fenimore Cooper
Cried: "Brothers!"
Everyone remembered Kosciuszko.
In Paris, Mickiewicz
Was eloquent: "The West,"
He said, "It dies of its doctrines!"
With Michelet and Quinet,
They cast him in bronze.
Of Lamennais: "He weeps for men."
Of Napoleon: "Come!"

Divination by Jacksonian Hickory:
Buchanan liked his ambassadorship,
His high teas with the Tzar.
In spite of Samuel Morse, that
Established Gomulka.
Churchill said: "It's no
Time for quarrels . . ."
Sikorsky crashed in his plane.
"Hel falls," said Hemar.
"Assassins steal our Westerplatte."

Batory, they've thrown your best
Philosopher out of Warsaw.
The one who stenographically took
The Devil's report.
I don't think Rosa Luxemburg
Would be pleased. She,
Like you, was a fighter & proud.

I like to think of Rilke's Angels
And his loving explanations to von Hulewicz.

I don't think about Esterhazy
Or Chopin. I think of Hass's poem
For his Polish friends in Buffalo.
Hass—who reads Mickiewicz
For his mushrooms.

I think of Jean Rousseau: "At least
Do not allow them to digest you!"
I think of Kazimierz Stanislaw Gzowski—
Knighted by Victoria, founder
Of the city of Toronto.
I think of Materski in the forests
Of my native Ohio: "Send no
Exiles inland." Ohio—unaware
Of 1830, of 1848.

Calling for my gambling debts,
The learned Purser
Quotes for me a famous
Unacknowledged source in Yiddish:
"Oh, frayg nit: 'Vus iz it?'
Los mir gehn zu machen Visit."

We approach the Gulf of St Lawrence.

Ten

The long aerial of Alma's German radio brings in, at last, the news. The C.B.C. is pleased: Nixon quits. That man named Gerald Ford is president. "An honest Nixon," someone says. "A sort of Hoover type." A little late, I think, for Hoover now. But we are on the river, the sun will surely rise, and very few are interested in politics. An age of boredom dawns. New Poland steams toward Old Quebec.

> I gather friends around me in
> The eerie morning haze:
> "'Sea hunger,'" I say, "'has gripped
> The West. It will hack its way
> To the Atlantic.' Friends,
> I'd have rather written that
> Than take the town. There died Wolfe
> Victorious. 'Let us build,' said
> Eisenhower, 'a canal!'

> "*Franciscus Primus,*
> *Dei Gratia Francorum Rex.*
> What, bearing such
> A cross, did Cartier observe?"

Indians, I suppose. Exotic birds. Looking for Cathay, he didn't hear, his German aerial extended to its length, such twitterings as these: 'I want to talk with you about what kind of line to take: I now what Kleindienst on it—It isn't a matter of trust. You have clearly understood that you will call him, give him the directions. I don't want to go off now to get us: ah! To maken ani deeeeeeeeals.'

Indians. And exotic birds. At sea there is no time, and therefore do ye joke about solemnities. Therefore do ye sip Courvoisier or ponderously lie, or sleep with other people's wives. But on a river? On a waterway that Eisenhower built? *Was ist Ihre Name,* after all? Open your Mickiewicz. Abandon your panjandrum. Suffer, when the hum of screws abates, your sea return.

On one arrival here the crew abandoned ship: engineers and deck hands diving through the portholes, swimming toward the haunted isle of Parkman's Marguerite. Thevet the cosmographer at Natron heard *her* tale. Polish seamen didn't. Instead of *Little*

Big Man, Warsaw played *Dziady* on a Forefather's Eve. George Sand had found it stronger stuff than *Faust.* Gomulka sent his tanks against the Czechs.

> Am I guilty of obscure
> Complicities, America? O Poland?
> The ugly birthright of
> My sinking class? Western
> Nations dress themselves
> To dream a dull apocalypse
> While I float down that
> River loved by old Champlain
> And every last Algonquin
> In his long canoe. I'm guilty
> And in luck in lousy times.

I walk the promenade deck, look at archipelagos and tiny fishing villages, return Mickiewicz to his shelf between the propaganda and the porn. I slip my bookmark, Jessie's letter dated just about a year ago, into a jacket pocket. Then I take it out and read it once again. "These few lines," she says, "to let you hear from me. I am up but I am havin trouble with my arm an shoulder pains me like before. But I was glad to hear from you an I am glad you all are well. I thought about you all because you did say you was

> Comin over before leavin an I
> Didn't know what happen. I don't
>
> Know whats wrong with people now an
> I'm afraid to set out on the porch
>
> Any more. Give my love to the girls
> An write me again some time. This
>
> Will be all for now. It's real
> Cold here. Love from your friend,
>
> Jessie Harris."

The
Mihail Lermantov
Poems

for Diana

Dogeared Proem: in which I decide to change my name before returning to England on a Russian ship after two years of sincerely trying to come to terms with America

Once I had a Polish friend, Zymierski.
He changed his name to Zane.
Dane Zane it became. (It's Zane Grey I blame.)
Perhaps you've seen his ivory-handled cane
In the historical museum
In Barcelona, Spain.
I resolved, in disapproval,
Never to change my name—
Even for the best of reasons,
Even in the worst of times,
Even for the sake of love, the sake of fame.

Still, today I've heard it claimed
The Baltic Shipping Company's
Investigating all the old Decembrists.
Safety first, I say.
Anyway, like Pushkin,
I'm interested in my maternal side.
(My father's fathers I cannot abide.)
No curly hair, no swarthy
Abyssinian face, I can't embrace
An Ibrahim (Great Peter's Black,
In lace); nor, like his
Successor Lermontov, find
My line extends to Ercildoune
And gnomic Thomas with his elves.
But I can reach for names
That suit me just the same

Like old Arzeno, watchmaker
And jeweler, born in some Italian drain,
Republican and Methodist
(Rare, as the obituary read,
For one of his nativity)
Who, once he reached Ohio
"Enjoyed the largest gains
In all of Georgetown"—

And Kirkpatrick, Scottish-Irish Democratic
Miller who was Abolitionist before
The Civil War, him whose
Moniker my social-working Aunt
Still answers to
In hot unsociable and palmy
Mid-Floridian lanes.
Her Christian handle's Jean,
Not Jane.

Arzeno and Kirkpatrick! How happily
I'd hyphenate your names!
Great grandfathering immigrants
Might summon if combined
In just proportions
A Maternal Spirit
Powerful as any Abyssinian or Elf
To whom I would declaim
A strange refrain:

—"O wild Italian-Irish Lass & Muse
O take aim and snipe at
(If not slay)
The heavy and judicial German
In me called Matthias.
Protect with *sprezzatura*
And some Gaelic gall this voyager
His life
His children and his wife.
O help me put on my disguise.
Help to make me good
And wise.
I'll be to God and man
Jack Arzeno-Kirkpatrick
For an odd span
Of days
Of days and nights."

Two

I'm introduced to the distinguished touring poet. He's a grand sight, all right. I'm mightily impressed. Dark hair, dark complexion, dark and piercing eyes. His companion (from the Secret Police? is our artist on a leash?) remarks with irritation: "Watch him. He will gaze contemptuously at all around him. He will greet you," the companion maintains, "with an unfriendly stare; he will be rude, insolent, and arrogant; he will respond, if he responds at all, to any remark of your own, with a sharp retort." I look at him and say: "You happen in one hidden glorious hour to waken in the longtime silent soul once more mysterious virgin springs of power." He responds with a sharp retort. I say: "Then trust them not? nor let their song be heard? Veil them in dark oblivion once again?" *In measured verse and icy rigorous words: a sharp retort.*

So. We understand one another immediately. With a little quick maneuvering in and around the more exotic midwestern towns we manage to lose his shadow somewhere in the vicinity of French Lick, Indiana. We fall immediately into a discussion of his life and times. "Bad times," he says. "Hard life." "Boring," he says. "Repressive." I smile sympathetically. "Listen," he says. "Nicky the First, after all! The Gendarme of Europe, The Cop. I exist at the will or the whim of a Cop." I smile sympathetically. "Monroe," I reply, "and his Doctrine. It's late applications. Not to mention Tzar Andrew—his powers & pains." He says: "The elegant and Jacobin Spring of December failed when I was young." "Yes," I sigh. "I remember the weather." And he: "The face of Pushkin." And I: "The fate of Poe." He buys me a Vodka Collins. In my imagination we are transported to Tsarkoie Selo where the poet, Cornet of the Life Guard Hussars, entertains. Saber blades, as Viskovaty has described the scene, "serve as standards for the sugar-heads which, with rum poured over them, burn with a beautiful blue fire, poetically lighting the drawing room from which for the sake of effect all candles have been removed."

"I became famous in a single day," he tells me after a couple of drinks. "Anna Mihailovna Hitrovo—we knew her as *la lèpre de la société*—showed that angry poem of mine to the Tzar. 'Fuel for revolution' she told the greedy crew that round his sceptre crawled. They sent me to the Nijegorodsky Dragoons where I slept in the open fields to the howling of jackals. I ate *churyok,* drank Kakhetian wine, and dressed like a Circassian with a gun in my belt. Still, Bielinsky praised the 'iron clangour' of my mighty line, and the mountains were a consolation." Abruptly, he stops. After a long and awkward silence, he blows out the sweet smelling and eerie blue-burning sugar heads of my imagination. "Do you like the sea?" he enquires. "You'll perish, of course, in a duel."

He heads east in a '73 Datsun. He turns into a ship.

Three

Ah, the stuff of greatness: Lermontov! Lermontov!
And the sources of greatness, Pushkin
And Byron. A lecture on greatness: by Olga
Our cultural commissar. An example
Of greatness, contemporary: our captain, Aram Mihailovich.
A great weight: the 20,000 tons of our ship.
A great mountain range: the Caucasus.
Great is the sauna, the caviar, the vodka
And the Volga: great is the Volga Boatman, the boatman
Himself and the song in his honour.
The bridge is great, the ballroom is great,
The bars are great (and the booze in the bars): also
The bilgewater is great and the bureaus
In the Bureaucracy: great are the drawers
Of each bureau, the pencils and papers inside,
The paper-clips and the pens.
Great is the promenade deck and the number three hatch.
Leningrad is a great city.
Moscow is a great city. The Odessa steps are
Great steps, especially in the film
By Eisenstein, the great Russian director.
A Russian passenger tells me
In the gym: "Our system is greater than yours!"
Great is the gym, the barbells and the jumping ropes:
These will make us strong! The waiter pours
Us at breakfast endless glasses
Of pineapple juice: these will make us strong.
Marx will make us strong. Lenin will make us strong.
Great & strong is the ghost of Engels
Far away in the ruins of Birmingham mills
And great is our chief engineer, Vasily Vasilyevich,
Who runs the engines turning propellers
Made by the great propeller makers of Leningrad.
Great is the Neva River and the drawbridge across it
The Winter Palace the Rostral Column the gate
Of Mihailovsky Garden the Admiralty the Palace Square
And Isaac's Cathedral, all of these sights

To be seen on a tour of the great city of Leningrad.
Great is cyrillic calligraphy
And beautiful too in the hands of ancient scribes
Who lived in ancient abodes before our own glorious times.
Great are our own glorious times
And great are the writers of our own glorious times
Their works and their days. Great is
The writers' union and Ivan Ivanovich its guiding spirit
And great patriotic example:
Great are his works:
Especially great are his volume of poems *Praise*
To The Combine Harvester and his novels
Bazooka and *Love in a Sewage Treatment Facility.*
Great is the port side of the ship
And the starboard, great is the fore and the aft,
Great is the bow and the bowsprit
And the Bow of Rostropovich its resin and hairs:
Great too is Shostakovich, sometimes:
His greatness appalls us in his Leningrad Symphony
If slightly less in his decadent earlier works
And his very private string quartets.
Great without doubt is the Bolshoi Ballet all the time
And great are the fountains
Of Peter the Great who was certainly great
In his time
And in his time a progressive.
Great is my cabin
Cabin 335
Where I read an anthology
Full of English and American poems
In Russian
And find in juxtaposition
One by Kenneth Koch
And one by Stephen Spender
And think continually
And think continually of what is great.

Four

I

And I have broken my resolution to stick it out in America. I said I'd suffer sea return, abandon my Panjandrum. I made some very solemn public promises in *TriQuarterly* magazine, Number 35: Yes, Bielinsky, in the famous *Stefan Batory Poems,* written on another ship, heading in the opposite direction. Stern and manly verses, iron clanging, yea! in every line. Readers world-wide are asking: Did I ever see Mrs. Harris again? How is Michelson doing? What became of Kevin? Is Sandeen writing poems? How do I pronounce: Mickiewicz? *Mickiewicz?* And who is wise Lizdejko? And who is wise Printz-Påhlson? Have I been sued for plagiarism? Libel? I didn't, did I, change my name to Arzeno-Kirkpatrick for nothing.

> Dreary, gentle reader, were my days in Indiana;
> Drab beyond my dreams. Besides,
> My wife is British. She'd abandon me entirely
> If I didn't take her to England
> For the Bicentennial Year.

> Also, I've had troubles with a lovely lady student.
> Whose wrath, you see, I flee. *"vi sva-BOD-ni
> s'i-VOD'-n'e V'E-chi-rem?"* I asked, though in English. *What?*
> *"DAY-t'i mn'e vash A-dr'is."* Who?
> ("Possession of an innocent, an unfolded soul,"
> Says Lermontov's Pechorin: "Boundless delight!")
> "Maybe I'm too old for this," I told her in the night.
> "Hath delight," she cried, "its bounds and bonds?
> "Doth brilliant Abelard just fall to bits in flight?"

> "Which bits are falling?" I enquired.

II

> England! Which bits are falling? *What?*
> In Dunwich
> And in Dunkirk.
> *What?*

Will there always be an England
Now that Wilson's out
Now that there's a drought in Suffolk?
Sings Callaghan, P.M., waking up
At Number Ten to pour
The North Sea Oil on his Kraut:
God bless the god bless the godblessed Yanks.
O help us sell our tanks
To somebody, thanks!

We know the Saudis want the Tower.
Already
Arabs own the Dorchester
And Royal Kens-
Ington Hotels. They hold controlling
Interest in the Cotswolds
And the Fens.
Nigeria is going to want the Inns of Court.
Castles reassemble daily
In our dreams
In dirty streets in Cairo and Uganda.
Better they should grow
On rocky California coasts. Better
Move the Bank of England into Berkeley or Big Sur.
Better ship the Bodleian to Boston or New York.
Who, after all,
Saved the battle field at Hastings? *What?*
Bought the bloomin' battle field for Blighty. *What?*
Better that a worthy bridge
Should span a tract of Arizona desert sands
Than sink into the Thames
Or fall into the hands & vanish in the lands of

To Mister K said Mister Nix
I want to see a little symmetry of islands
in the sticks
both east and west of us.
I've got a little fix on certain stars
tells
which island, Baby,
maybe
's gonna be
of States the 51st of 'em
in one
nine seven
six.

Five

I carry with me once again: the mail.
There is, after all, nearly always
Mail to chasten or to cheer—(it reached me
This time in New York)—and there are two
Classes of friends: those who write
When one's away
And those who don't or won't.

Says Joe: "As an added attraction in my dreams last night, there was a letter from you at the end of which was an addendum in red ink. The writing was large, spacious, and very lucid. It was some sort of a note from your wife, but it was signed: "Cissy" (?). Suddenly the three of us were in an open motorboat cruising through the Everglades, accompanied by a group of people called "The Mini-Multi Nations": Each person was dressed most luridly in his native garb, and each, in turn, sang the folksongs of his native land in native lingo. There was a German on board, complete with green Alpine cap and burly legs, on whom the whole group turned when it came to be his time to sing. As we proceeded up the river, another, smaller motorboat crossed our bow. There were two fishermen in it, and one of them, quite ugly, cast his line into our boat, dragging the German out of it and into the water. Anyway, I'm writing letters to graduate schools and wondering: Have I got a chance at Heidelberg?"

Was muss man tun um ein guter Seeman zu sein.
What to do to be a good sailor.
Wenn Sie sich unwohl fühlen, müssen Sie sich im Ferien in der
    frischen Luft bewegen, mit etwas beschäftigen, und wenn
    Sie irgend können-etwas essen.
If you feel ill, keep moving and busy in the fresh air; this will
    often drive away dizziness and save you the not so good
    experience of MAL DE MER.

From an anonymous informant: the news that, in my absence, I have been the victim of a parody and mock-panegyric by a certain (clearly pseudonymous) N. Talarico published in a local (to the bush) but most notorious little mag. I am sent quotations from the choicest bits of his encomium: "To Matthias, as He Makes A Name For Himself." He begins, himself, with a quote: ". . . not unlike Darwin playing the trombone to his French beans." My portrait ("Sir, the subject is mean—like Eustace Budgel who threw himself into the Thames") follows at once: "Weary hair that sprawls like a hanging garden of King Neb's grass, vaulted forehead, wrinkles, fluting, proud dripping eyes, the schizoid clergyman buried under one too many vows . . . nerves frizzing and popping like the ectoskeleton of some prodigious frying crustacean. . . ." But I cannot go on.

Patty writes: "I told McMurphy and McBride I was going to invite you to become a Catholic and they *hooted*. So I won't but still I think it's what we have to offer. Phytophthora root rot infests your pseudopodium. I saw Solzhenitsyn on TV; it was apocalyptic. *I* was apoplectic, afraid for the first time. I have something wrong with a bone in my foot. Stop drooling in self-pity, I tell myself. Face it, this is your home. Why do you keep going away? Think of McMurphy and McBride. I wanted to hide and am hiding but now I want to be found.

Who do you think has a death wish?
Have a good year, boss, truly.
Regards. The end.
Olé.
Patty."

Around and about. With the girls, first,
For haircuts. Less is more, as someone said,
And Cynouai looks ravishing
And two years older with her long hair
Shorn by Russian barberesses & skinny male apprentice.
Laura watches skeptically, then
Wants short hair too.
Two babushkas, says a barberess, blushing.
We say thanks, *spasiba*. We pay in roubles, smile,
And walk the decks. At a kiosk: safety pins
And toothpaste. At a coffee lounge: espresso, strong.
Smooth sea, clear sky: you can see for miles.
I think to myself: I am happy.
It is not our lot to be happy. I say to
My wife: though you know that I know it is not our lot
To be happy, today, I say, I am happy.
Today, she says, you are foolish.
Propaganda shorts, punctuated by cartoons,
Begin in the Rainbow Cinema at ten.
Their approach is not unlike my own: This is
The city of Moscow. See the happy people. See them
Work and play. Though we know you know
We know it is not their lot to be happy, today, we say,
They are happy. Today I can almost believe it.
Olga says: Some of you on board
Do evidently take my elementary Russian classes
Lightly. Therefore there will be, she adds,
Examinations. Rossiya, we learn today,
Is from Slavonic
Rus or Ros
Which is from Rutosi which is Finnish
Meaning Swedes
A corruption for the Swedish Rothsmenn
Meaning seamen meaning rowers
Meaning rowers rowing
Seamen
Back to Rothsmenn

To Rutosi Russ or Ross
Slavonic Rossiya. We continue. We row on.
Though we're not permitted visits to the engine room
We are very welcome, thank you, in the galley.
Why, I wonder, as we gaze upon
The shining copper bottoms of the many pots and pans.
Our master cook is called Natasha. First assistant: Fred.
Says Natasha brightly: *SUP n'i-da'SO-l'in:*
There is too little salt in the soup.
Gangs of rival youths, the spoiled sons
Of diplomatic families, East & West, cavort in narrow
Hallways, make a passage dangerous.
We disapprove of gangs of rival youths. We approve
Of peaceful placid crossings always in all seasons yes indeed
And fully air conditioned, stabilized.
We disapprove: of television, of atomic power,
Of planes. We approve: of solar energy, of poetry,
Of ships. Beep beeps of daily news
Are amplified through all the hidden speakers in the walls.
There's no escaping it, nor the *Aurora,* tabloid version
Of the same. Reagan shouts: Remember the Main.
(Does he know about the Storozhevoy?)
In the Commons, fisticuffs; the Pound is down
To one point six. Carter's got his democratic delegates:
He'll win the nomination. Ford will have to fight.
We disapprove: of Carter, Ford, and Reagan. We approve:
Of George the Third and Pitt.
Up on deck again. Sea gulls off the stern:
There must be islands near. At our feet, heavy ropes
And chains for tying up in ports.
Cynouai sights serpent which she likens unto lobster.
Balistae, she has read, threw Regulus his army
At such an awesome shape as this.
She quotes us Olaus Magnus: ". . . . rising like a mast
And eating sheep and swine disturbing ships
And snapping angry men from slippery decks . . ."
Cynouai's developed in the last two years
Some devastating Indiana playground jive—charms
And spells & incantations—which, lamentably,
She teaches gentle Laura. Their poetry
Is ancient and confounding: it ruins equally the
Innocent and guilty, wrecking the unwary.
They smile sweetly at the little boy at lunch

Who has expressed enthusiasm for his broccoli.
"So, so, suck your toe!/All the way to Mexico!"
He pales and expires in his parents' arms.
We vainly offer consolation.
Who among the passengers, we wonder,
Represents the K.G.B.?
Shall we forgive the K.G.B. its agent
On our ship? That wizard in the game room
Taking on all comers at the chess board,
That's the one. Or the strange aristocratic
Lady we discovered after midnight
On the upper deck where animals are kept in kennels
Who was feeding her pet bat.
I notice on a printout that the management
Declines to be responsible
For Acts of God or Piracy (that's fair);
Or for quarantines and seizures, strikes
And "latent vice." They reserve the right
To "land" us if the Captain thinks we are obnoxious
Or unfit. So says clause fourteen;
And I wonder how obnoxious we can get before
We're landed, how they make that nice
Distinction about latent vice.
After lunch, the girls swim.
I talk a while to Brad, a Unitarian from Cleveland,
About sin. I complete some customs forms
And see the big-armed baggage boss. I think of
Olga Korbut, do some exercises in the gym.
Deckspiele, Bridgespiele, if we want to play,
Can bring us prizes: Russian furs
And Balalaikas for the winners. Tea is in
The Vostok Lounge today. Dancing lessons are at four.
The little tailor promises to press
Diana's wrinkled evening dress.
Our Master, Aram M. Oganov, cordially invites us
To attend a formal cocktail party
In the Large Saloon where he will introduce
His senior colleagues late this afternoon. The orchestra
Will play, and Leonid Bozokovich will sing.
Mihail Lermontov, will they recite your poems?
I doubt it, friend. The Baltic Shipping Company and crew
Don't know your stuff, I fear, though
Curiously enough they still have uses for poet's

Name and legend in the end.
The legend is extreme.
When you died, the locals exorcized your house.
The incense suffocated every flea & louse.
Terrified,
They thought you were demonic.
But you were only just
                   a little bit
                          Byronic.

Seven

My sympathy extends to Lord George-Brown whose photograph is printed in *Aurora* having toppled over in the street outside the B.B.C. in London where he had appeared, more than just a little drunk, to be interviewed and to destroy, before the grinding cameras, his Labour Party card. He was very moved, he said, to do this thing. Then he slipped and fell.

Once I met George Brown, when he was Foreign Secretary, at a party given by my future in-laws shortly after I'd been smitten by the beauty, brains, and grace of a certain elegant Miss Adams. In heady company, in the middle of the mythic Sixties, a decade when intensities were commonplace and inspiration was the rule, my head made light, my tongue made loose by many minty gins, I asked Miss A. to marry me. That I had a wife at home already didn't, at the time, seem to be a complication. I was moved, I said, like Lord George-Brown, to do this thing. Then I slipped and fell.

A few months earlier, Diana blew her interview with M.I.5. What can you do, after all, with a degree in Russian from an English Tech if you're fastidious and will not spy? Her regular attendance at the London branch of the Russian Orthodox Church, as girl chorister, alarmed them as they positively vetted her. She sang, angelic, with a group of ancient (indeed Tzarist) emigrés she'd met at Holborn College. But, ah! who else, wondered M.I.5, might one meet at such a place of dubious repute and mysteries? Their suspicions ended abruptly what might have proved to be a distinguished career. Diana was a pious sort for a while, and took me off to what we later started calling "smells and bells." Once in an endless Sunday mass I scribbled in frustration on an envelope: "O Flaming Slavic God, I pray / Cooperate with me today / Undo this chastity, I say!" It was January, then, of 1967. It took Him roughly until May. . . .

Eight

Hydrodynamics, brother:
waves, and what? makes? waves?
Who or how, then, poets,
oh! the ships. Of similitude
and crest lines, cusps:
We sing it, Mihail Yurievich,
together, no?
For English *scip,* sir,
German *schiff:* all root-like *skap*
I deal I dig out *scoop:*
Scop, we say it, lad, and
ship-shape: poet!
who hath scope enough?
by means of which (of whom) doth
man contrive, convey himself & goods upon
the waves, who waves at
signals lovingly what wives
await returning man he
shanty sings of sea-born signs
Armada Ajax Agamemnon
lo! Renoun or Devastation, *ho—*
Potemkin Homer Mayakovsky
Virgil quote: "Then
first the rivers hollowed alders felt!"

But what? makes waves? components
of Resistance: poets
must, as ships do, dear, encounter
counter, count on it:
so resonant these waves
this hull our hallmark, helmsman—
Red or restive
forces vary as their masses
Newton said of similitude a principle
vouchsafe it I to
poets ships of state or captains
legislators unacknowledged

wonder (I do) *could* you, Lermontov,
have suffered out an exile
in "The West?"
In my America, "America"
in circumstances
we could hypothetically
imagine for you
tired and poor
and brave
and staring down some shitfaced
bureaucrat who couldn't
spell your name
on Ellis Island though it
wouldn't have been
Ellis Island then, not yet?
Instead of death at 26
an immigration
maybe
to ByGod ByGum
your ship against
our waves
your waves against
our shores
resistance or combustion and collapse?

Napoleon abdicates
and Washington burns down.
Clay, Calhoun
and Crawford clamour.
Madison makes war.
Who'd mediate with Castlereagh?
Who'd cluck: "The Tzar?"
Commission oh commissioner it's
Adams fast and far.
Francis Key goes spangley in a decent dawn.
Thornton saves the patents.
You blink
at Moscow midwives
and you learn to say: Tarhani.
Your generation's made superfluous
in Russia by
the poet-peacock's frenzy
of December '25: the profiles

of the hanged
bleed into the margins of *Onegin.*
As the dandy and the duelist
replace the likes of
Kuchelbecker and Kondraty Ryleev,
the Masons go all misty
and Mickiewicz cries: despair.

Do I see you as a Locofoco candidate?
An alien-seditious Natty Bumppo
tough enough to topple even Tammany?
Or Bard of Biddle's Bank?
Cousin, your ambivalence about all things
matches even mine:—
You take, I think,
no Hannibalic oath with Herzen.

On the Wabash, maybe,
some reformer leads you
as a pre-pubescent
to anticipate Pechorin's adolescence
with the Shaker image
of a rehabilitated bum
coined in Owen's dialogues
with Adams & Monroe:
A Hero Of Our Time in Indiana,
positive & realist,
wrought to win in 1841
the Brook Farm Fourier award,
wrought to win
the distant praises of Zhadanov.

"Oh the plundered plowman
and the beggared
yeomanry," quoth Jefferson
who never really cared about
the buggered beggers—
And old John Randolph said: "it's
a stinking coalition now
of Blifil and Black George!"
Bargain and intrigue, he meant,
between the Nullifiers
and the Feds.

Though you were only twelve,
who hath scope enough?
In time, perhaps,
you'd be a good Jacksonian:
A kitchen-cabinet member
cribbing notes from Crockett
pilfering from Poe
dreaming of Tecumseh's ghost
and Lake Ontario
as you give your arm, chivalrous,
to the blemished Peg O'Neale,
write your epic *Alamo*
and draft at last a swan song
in your famous
ode: "Hypothicated Bonds."

In 1837, with the Panic,
you take off:
The West! You write to Mme. Arsenieva
née Stolypin: "The Rockies
are my Caucasus in exile:
who hath scope enough?" And of
the river boats: "*The means!* by which
a man contrives—
conveys himself and goods
upon the waves . . ."
All the rest is lost in mountain mists
and in
the numberless lacunae
which I find
in Olga's reading lists.

Oh, you were born beneath a curious star.
Who'd mediate with Castlereagh
would cluck: "The Tzar."
I whisper in your dreamy ear
babushka
in your favorite hatch.

We heave most handily past headlands toward the Thames.

Nine: A Conclusion of The Mihail Lermontov Poems beginning with documentation, paraphrase, and quotations taken down in the Revolutionary Reading Room from a fine old tome on the Thames by Allen Wykes and ending by way of a change, once again, of my name . . .

At the other end of the river, at the other end of time, they offer sacrifices to the Great God Lud: a bevy of virgins is flushed down the spring at Lechlade where the River God and his friends—who much prefer the virgins to the sheep and roosters which they sometimes get instead, a substitution which, as we can easily imagine, often leads to wicked floods in the Spring—run (says my authority) *a pumping station belching out the daily fifteen hundred million gallons of water* pouring toward us even now over the weir at Teddington as we flow west with the tide toward Tilbury. *Hic tuus O Tamisine Pater septemgeminus fons:* "Here, O Father Thames, is your sevenfold fount." Among the potamologists, in fact, there is no agreement as to exactly where it is. But Leche will do for us as it did for Drayton in his *Polyolbion,* as it did for his friend Shipton when he found in Trewsbury Mede that "no water floweth hereabouts til Leche, the onlie true begetter."

> *If to my starboard red appear*
> *It is my duty to keep clear;*
> *Act as judgement says is proper*
> *Port or starboard—*
> *Back or stop her . . .*

None of your *Wallala-leialalas* for us; that's a boatman's song with a social function to perform. Not so long ago the captains of ships mismanaged by members of the lively fraternity operating out of Gravesend under the Ruler of Pilots were encouraged to dispatch on the spot any incompetent or unlucky helmsman with appropriate ceremonials or without. We've flown our yellow Q and blue and orange stripes; we've blown an angry short and two long blasts on our horn and taken on our pilot from the pilot cutter. He sings his lonely song: *But when upon my port is seen/a steamer's starboard light of green,/For me there's nought to do or see/that green to port keeps clear of me.* So we are now in the hands of a specialist in rivers and can hope, muttering whatever spells or mnemonics we like, to reach our proper berth with no encounters along the way with any supertankers, QE 2s, ghostly Kelmscott oarsmen, estuary chains, Gordon fortifications, sunken Armadas, lightships, sands, sheers, nesses, muds, or stone outcroppings along the Hundred of Hoo. The statue of Pocahontas, who never made it home, stares at us through a Dickensian fog.

"His body doth incarnadine," remarked a jailor, "Thamesis to uncommon sanguine beauty." It was a notable execution. If Thames Head is hard to find—whether in the Mede or in the Leche or in the Pool at Seven Springs—the Thames heads are far too numerous to count.

I see them vividly before me bobbing in our wake, all those lovely saints and sinners, chatting with each other about noble or ignoble deeds, drifting toward Westminster with the tide. That it should have been the *head* that always so offended! Why not, like Montezuma, pluck out hearts? No, the English god did not want hearts; you lose your head or mind in this cold country, or you hang. Your heart is yours for hoarding. Said the Virgin Queen, keeping hers to herself, red of wig and black of tooth, Tilbury protectress—"I have the heart and stomach of a king!" The pirate Drake prepared once more to burn the Spanish beard:—*with*
further protestatione that if wants
of victualles and munitione were suppliede we wold
pursue them to the furthese
that they durste
have gone . . .
A less official pirate, late of Scotland, said most memorably upon espying, there on execution dock, a friend: "I've lain the bitch three times and now she comes to see me hanged!" Three tides washed the bones; then he waved for days from Bugsby's Reach. . . . Tippling pints in Whitby's Prospect or in Ramsgate's Town we think we'd like it better in the past. When they flushed the virgins down the drain at Leche, floated heads in rivers or impaled them ornamentally on pikes—when oh they hung the pirates low beneath the tide.
We'd drink we would we'd
go pursue them durste
supply the victualles and munitione
write immortal doggerel we'd fight for Gloriana
Boudicca Victoria Regina choose your time
by Kitchener do your bit
for Winston spot the doodlebugs and buzzbombs
pluck out mines off Cliffe
outfox De Ruyter beat that prick Napoleon
prop on some dark night
a poor unlucky scapegoat in the new foundations my fair lady
of the bridge
and bind him there
we'd set a man to watch all night we'd do the job ourselves.
But you do not choose your time.

Lucky, guilty—
exiled or pursued,
some can choose at least a place.
As the times impinged
obscurely, George Learmont abandoned Thomas Rhymer's tower and—as mercenary, pirate—left his home and went to organize the cavalry in Poland for a minor Tzar. His business there was doubtless foul. Later, Mihail Yurievich would dream of heather, kilts,

and thistles, dream of George Learmont, dream of ancestors and Malcolm and MacBeth as time—his times—impinged on him obscurely, making him superfluous, sending him to the Dragoons and to the mountains where he prophesied his end, with great precision, twice. He "eloquently yearned," a learned scholar writes, quoting his worst stuff, "to fly to high and misty crags and wake the wild harp of Scotland once again." But the Russian god, unlike the English, wanted hearts, great hearts—Lermontov's and Pushkin's—a nasty bullet through each one. The Russian god would make of both a statue and a ship—machinery converting poetry to prose, roubles into dollars, treaties into grain, and revolution into resolutions and détente. Because of which we may avoid a holocaust and bore each other to our graves.

> For my time, too, impinges oddly,
> painlessly, obscurely—this kind of inbetween—
> impinges surely
> this time of jokes & parodies, pastiches.
> An inbetween
> when I don't know precisely what I want to do in time
> but only where I want to go
> again—
> And so we're here and waiting
> for a berth
> to park a ship in—
> waiting in a time of waiting
>
> A time of waiting for—
> For semi-retired former semi-active veteran-volunteers
> of oh our still belovéd
> dear and hopeful
> sixties
> to arise again arise
> again arise
> For some kind fool to build the equestrian statues
> and compose the elegiac songs.
>
> Riding high and mightily on weary white lame mare
> whose forelegs beat the air
> and haunches heave
> his head at a tilt, his purple pluméd hat all brandishéd
> on high on high
> on point of keen upraiséd terrible swift sword
> Squadron Leader Jack Arzeno-Kirkpatrick
> sings his able arias

in honour of Air Vice-Marshal Matthias—
who has children
and a wife
who is middle class for life.

Said Marx (correctly):
men will make their history, all right,
but not exactly
as they think or choose.
(Even he had everything to lose
with that excuse.)

The signal flags unfurl and fly;
the lights flash on.
Down come blue and orange stripes,
the yellow Q:
Up go W and L, and
up goes V:
Have you got dead rats on board?
Answers ATI: *There is no cause for alarm.*
BCV replies: *Approved.*
Down come quickly *rats, no cause, approved*—
Up goes HKB:
*Hello, Komsomolka: I want
to ask you a question. Is gallantry obsolete?*
Flaps the dreaded Drake: *Think, by god,
of the Queen.* Down with HKB
and Drake, up with
M. Maksimich: *Was it the French who invented
the fashion of being bored?*
We fly the blue Pechorin: *No, it was the English.*
Taking our various oaths, we resolve
to be gallant again, and brave—
yes, Komsomolskaya—
and away with Boredom, England!
We fly *The Plundered Plowman.*
We will not plunder—
we'll plow.
We fly *The Beggared Yeoman.*
We will not beggar
we'll yodel.
And there's a kind of waterish Tree at Wapping

whereat sea-thieves
or pirates are catched napping.

Oh, our resolutions are serious enough
in spite of the jokes
and in spite of our preoccupations
—the baggage, the passports—
and we really do propose to lead a better life this year
than last
though we do not tell ourselves exactly how.

Standing on the promenade
in attitudes
of suspicion, attention, or anticipation
hoping for some fine
benign surprise
each of us looks at the land
thinking still of the sea.
Each contrives
to be abstracted one last time in sea-thoughts
or in dreams
before the symbolical stranger
posing as a customs agent
or a clerk or porter in a small hotel or pension
asks the question symbolical strangers ask
which only actions answer

and each, I think, hums a variation
on the final chorus
of the tune
—changing names and faces,
touching all the graces—
that he's whistled up and down the decks
through afternoon & afternoon.

—O wild Italian-Irish Lass & Muse
protect with sprezzatura
and some Gaelic gall this voyager
his life
his children and his wife.
O help me take off my disguise.
Help to make me good
and wise.

I've been to God and man
Jack Arzeno-Kirkpatrick
for an odd span
of days
of days and nights.

Northern Summer

For Joseph Buttigieg and Vincent Sherry

The flight of sentimentality through empty space.
Through its elliptical hole
an heraldic blackbird's
black wings, yellow beak, round eyes, with the yellow
ring, which defines its inner empty
space
                              —GÖRAN SONNEVI

I The Castle

                    Occupies
a picturesque
commanding strong position
on the summit of a cliff some forty
feet in height
the base of which is covered
up at flood tide by the waters of the Forth.
Large, magnificent, commodious
with rock nearby and wood and water to afford
the eye a picture of a rare
and charming beauty
forming a delightful and romantic spot
the sight of which
could not but amply compensate et
cetera
                    the language of a tour book
threading aimlessly
through sentimental empty space.

Or build on, say, an Edward's language
to his dear and faithful cousin
Eymar de Valance
like a second generation builds upon
the ruins of a first?

                    finding not

in our
Sir Michael Wemyss
good word
nor yet good service and
that he now shows himself in such a wise
that we must hold him traitor
and our enemy we do command you that ye
cause his manor where we lay
and all his other manors to be burned his lands
and goods to be destroyed
his gardens to be stripped all bare
that nothing may remain
and all
may thus take warning—

Language
moving upon consequence
Consequence
upon a language: Flight
of an heraldic bird
through space that is inhabited.

Some say Bruce had raised his standard here.

II   Pied-à-Terre

I live between the castle and the coal mine
in a folly. It's the truth.
They put a roof on it last year. I have
a room, a window on the sea.

                    Strange to say, I
haven't seen my host yet,
Captain Wemyss.
He's holed up in his castle in this awful rain.
I'm holed up in my folly with
my pads and pens.
If the sun comes out this month, maybe yet
we'll meet
a-walking in the garden O.

                    "Baron Wemyss of Wemyss"

94

all the old books call
his many forbears.
Do I just shout out *hello there
Wemyss of Wemyss?*
Seven centuries of purest Scottish pedigrees,
says Mr. F., the Edinburgh historian.
Twenty-seven generations.
I can offer
just one eighth of watery Kirkpatrick.

The flight of sentimentality through empty space!
A rhetoric, at least; (an awkward line).
The flight of Sentiment
is through a space that's occupied.

This space is occupied, all right,
and I am guest
of both the present and the past.

                    The past
begins in caves,
the Gaelic *Uamh* soon enough becoming Wemyss.
James the Fifth surprised
a band of gipsies in one cave, drinking there
and making merry. Though he
could join them incognito in his famous role
as Godeman of Ballangeich
and share their mad hilarity, James the Sixth
would only shout out *treason*
when he panicked of a sudden, claustrophobic,
in a *Uamh* become a mine.

Above the caves and mines they built this house.

And put a chaplain in it! I find there was
no piper here, and worse, no bard—
But Andrew Wyntoun, a prior of St Serf,
wrote a family chronicle in verse
& praised
                    *An honest knycht
and of good fame
Schir Jhone of Wemyss by his rycht name.*

Well, if I'm the guest of absent hosts
the cost of lodging here a while
is neither waived
nor anywhere within my calculation—
(the flight of Sentiment
is not
through empty space)

Did Mynyddog Mynfawr, camped along the Forth,
feed the brave Gododdin mead and wine
a year
a year
a year?

Or did he send them sober down his mine?

III The Mine

The flight through empty space of Sentiment
—mentality! There's nothing
sentimental
within sight of this abandoned mine.
From where I stand
I'd talk about dead gods, I think.
                           From where I stand on this
deserted beach
between the castle and the mine
I think I'd say the legates
of the dead god Coal
had built his image here to look
exactly like a gallows made of iron & alloy
high enough
to hang a giant from—

The tower's erect upon the hill, but nothing moves.

Who worked here once?
No Free Miners from the Forest of Dean
have hewn the coalface down the ages
here at Wemyss from when
the coughing grey-eyed servants

won the coal
for monks at prayer in freezing Dunfermline
but virtual slaves. No *gales,* no lease
for them.
                   "Coal beneath the soil
shall be inherited with soil
and property." The lairds of Fife could pack
a Privy Council and by act of law
reduce a man to serfdom. He
was bought or sold
along with his equipment. His child
went underground at six
to earn an extra seven pence
lest he sail to Noroway with Sir Patrick Spence.

The tower's erect upon the hill, and nothing moves.

When fire leapt down the tunnel, forked and dove,
an age had come and gone. The
nation voted Labour
but the coal board blundered here in Wemyss
at once.
                   The lift plunged down
through all that soaring iron and alloy, down
to where the caves and tunnels
smoulder uselessly and spread the fire
on inland through
bituminous rich veins. It could burn
a hundred years. It could burn as far as London.

Miles of heavy cable lie around me
on the beach. Almost ankle-thick, it unravels
like a length of rope left over
from a hanging. It raised and lowered the lift.
The lift descended with amazing speed.
With amazing speed
the fire leapt down the tunnel, forked and dove.
Everyone, I think, got out.

A tanker steams across the bleak horizon.

The tower's erect upon the hill.

IV A Queen

John Knox said the visit of the Queen
had raised the price
of wild fowl sufficiently
that patridges were sold at half a crown.
He was not a sentimental man.
Of the Regent's coronation
he'd remarked: "Seemly
as to put a saddle on the back
of an unruly cow."
                              O belle

et plus que belle crooned
Mary's friend, Ronsard. Better him than Knox
for gentle conversation?
Better all the Medicis & better maybe
little sick king Frank
whose inflammation of the middle ear
and abscess of the brain
were dear to Calvin.
                              And yet her keen eyes
danced out of a window here
in February, 1565.
It was cold that year in Fife.
Every fireplace here at Wemyss was blazing
full of fine Wemyss coal
when Mary gazed at Charles Darnley riding by.
Yesterday was warm & bright
when Peggy, who's the cook, pointed
out the window, showing me
where Darnley had dismounted. I had come
to get a pan to heat some water in.
He had come to woo a queen,
win the Matrimonial Crown and full equality
of Royal right, make every kind
of mischief in the realm. The empty space
between the window and
the place he stood beside his horse
in sexy tight black hose was filled at once
with Feeling—

Darnley sang a song more serious than Ronsard's
and Bothwell entered in his

little book that Kirk o'Field's convalescent
suffered from *roinole* and not
petite verole—
                 syphilis, not smallpox.
But that was later on.
At Wemyss it was a sentimental morning.

V A Prince

Or talk about Charles Edward then.
Charles, Edward, Louis,
Sylvester, Maria, Casimir, Stewart.
The Bonnie Prince himself,
the grand Chevalier. To the Forty-Five
this castle sent Lord Elcho.
Kindred of my own kin's forbears, my
brooding and attainted
absent host,
                 he gazed from Holyrood
through gilded ballrooms & out casement windows
at the gillies & the pipers & the clans
weighing odds, meditating
languages—Gaelic, French, the
lisped Italian English of his Regent Prince.

        The King enjoy his ain again?
Doubtful, but for honour
one must risk in any case this autumn theatre
although it issue
in a winter's desolation. . . .

Claymore!—
                 (or is it *Gardyloo?*)—echoes
even now from Holyrood
through Fife. Beneath those Strathspey
dancers' feet when Elcho's mother
led off celebrations
of the rout as Prestonpans,
history smouldered with surprises
older than the coal fields
on the Wemyss estate.
Language moved upon inconsequence

and consequence
at once: *Will you see me
to my quarters?* and

                    No quarter . . .

as if you'd hear two voices whispering
behind you while you stared
down Royal Mile thinking of the sheltered hollow
under Arthur's seat. . . .

The empty space between the window
framing Elcho and the place the clansmen camped
filled up in time with sentimental tales
and the progeny
of all those partridges
whose price the visit of the Scottish Queen
had raised, said Knox, to half a crown.
And yet his line of vision then
was tangent to
the flight of an heraldic bird
whose spiral into time
was on a furious northern wind—
vehement,
and with a terrifying sound.

VI   A Voice

I hear my mother's voice reading Stevenson—
or is it Scott? Someone's wandering lost
among the heather. I must be eight or nine.
I know I should be reading this myself,
but when I read the words the voice I hear
ceases to be hers. . . .

                    There is a space
I have not learned to fill
somewhere between printed marks and sounds
and I am lost in some way too
among the heather, frightened of the distances
when all I want to do is drift on lang
uage into dream. . . .

                    "Cha n'eil Beurl' agam . . ."
someone says, but I follow him

in any case on hands & knees in terror.
Have I got the silver button in my teeth?
Am I papered for the murder of that
Campbell back in Appin? We're through
the cleft, the Heugh of Corrynakiegh,
and now the moor: it's black and burned
by heath fires. Moorfowl cry.
The deer run silently away from us. . . .

Or am I underneath the castle of my enemy?
And is my enemy my only friend? I hear
the sentinel calling out in English
All's well, All's well
but we crawl off toward a hovel
made of stone & turf & thatch. There's
a fire inside, and over it a small iron pot.
The ancient crone who's stirring it
offers me a boiled hand
                                  to steal away
some gentleman's attention
from his Ovid . . . and pack him off to bed
with images to mingle
with his dreams, said R.L.S. to Baxter.
And Scott: that "laws & manners
cast a necessary colouring;
but the bearings, to use heraldic language,
will remain the same,
though the tincture may be different
or opposed. . . ."
                          Bearings . . . tincture . . .
Theft and Dream,
flight of an heraldic bird through language,
and my mother's voice.

Who are the Kirkpatricks? where is Abbotsford?
How can poor sick R.L.S., listening with
his Hoosier wife, hear off in Samoa "beaten bells"
from just across the Firth?

For a moment, laws and manners seem no
more than colouring. Charles Edward back in Paris
casts a medal of himself—*Carolus Walliae*
Princeps—and the future hangs

on messages delivered by the likes of
Alan Breck from men like Cluny
in his cage—
language moving upon consequence. . . .

But time has gone to live with
Waverleys and Balfours, with townies
like Rankeillor and his lowland lawyer ilk.
I am awake in Fife. I hear
the distant echoes of my mother's voice reading.
Sentiment's transfigured into history,
and history to sentiment.

VII Kirkcaldy

In Kirkcaldy one considers economics.
We need a dozen eggs. I leave my folly, catch
a bus near Wemyss, and walk around
this "old lang toun" that bears the name
of Mary's last defender.
Loyal old Kirkcaldy, last
support and stay of an unlucky queen,
scourge of Bothwell, keeper
of the craggy rock in Edinburgh
out of which your one-time friend John Knox
would pry you even with his
final fetid breath—
                              Linoleum?
In June
descendents of those Covenanters Cromwell shot
treat their jute with linseed oil
where William Adam, stone & lime Vanbrughian,
built in Gladney House
a Netherlandish lesson for his sons
and Adam Smith returned in early middle age
and wrote.

Did Elcho see young Robert Adam on the castle wall
where John Knox saw Kirkcaldy? each one
moving through the crystal chambers
of his mind to build more perfect measurements
before the cannon fired

of distances heraldic birds might fly,
language moving upon consequence
to say *Nobility,*
Salvation, Space?
                    When Adam left
Kirkcaldy grammar school
for Edinburgh, Smith enrolled at
Glasgow, never mentioning (when he
returned at forty-five) the Forty-Five.
"The workmen carry nails instead
of money to the baker's shop and alehouse.
The seat of empire should remove itself
to that part of the whole
contributing the greatest share to its support.
In sea-port towns a little grocer
can make forty-five percent upon a stock. Capitals
increased by parsimony
are diminished by misconduct, prodigality. . . ."
And not a word about the bonded miners
in the collieries & salt pits.

Economies! Those workmen died
in nailers' dargs to earn a casual footnote.
That parsimony made a bigot certain he was saved,
his neighbour rightly damned.
That seat of empire never moved;
its rebel colonies themselves became imperious.
Those country houses made by Adam and his sons
rose up with fortresses
they built at Inverness on orders straight
from Cumberland, which bled.

The smell of jute on linseed
stinks of deprevation: linoleum peels off floors
of little grocers in this town
where faces in the baker's shop and alehouse
thirst for darker oils
sucked up Shell, BP, and Exxon rigs
from underneath the bottom of the sea.

The Regent dragged Kirkcaldy from his rock
and hung him on the gallows Knox prepared him for:
face against the sun.

His blinded eyes beheld a crazy German
sitting firmly on a Stuart throne.
History gave William Pitt *The Wealth of Nations,*
the brothers Adam peel-towers & Fort George.

Beggared sentiment flew straight into the hills

VIII Ossian, etc.

And metamorphosed there in Ossianic melancholy.
James Macpherson heard, he said,
the howling of a northern wind; he heard old men
chanting through the night about the woods
of Morven; Selma filled, he wrote,
with names & deeds—Fingal's, Oscar's, Gaul's—
but languae threaded aimlessly through empty spaces
& through languorous dreams, *with rock nearby*
and wood and water to afford the eye
a rare and charming beauty, the sight of which
could not but amply compensate
admirers of the sentimental and the picturesque.
Where better read a "forgery" than in a folly?

And shall I like these poems
that David Hume defended when he found
the heroes' names authenticated
by an inventory of all the Highland mastiffs?
Napoleon did, who never heard of Dr Johnson,
but who carried *Fingal* into battle
imitating, now and then, with relish,
the Ossianic style in his memos & dispatches.
And Goethe, caught up in the turmoil
of his *Sturm und Drang,* built
the European Zeitgeist from a massive
mountain sadness caught in far Temora.
Staring at Macpherson's book,
they filled the emptiness before their eyes
with what they were.
                                        It was an age
of forgeries & fakes: Pretenders
old and young, gothic ruins in the garden,
memories of casket letters, padded

coats and powdered wigs. And while Macpherson
roamed the hills in search of Gaelic bards,
a London dealer named Buchanan
sold the Earl of Wemyss a phony Venus
signed *Van Dyck:* "the sight of which could
not but amply compensate," etcetera,
Buchanan whispered softly in the noble ear,
and rubbed his hands, and grinned.
Staring at the canvas on his castle wall,
the Earl filled the emptiness before his eyes
with what he thought he saw.

"The Erse Nation may be furious with Lord North,
for even Fingal tells him so,
but adds: 'And yet, my Lord, *I* do not
desert you.'" Walpole, 1782.
Macpherson travelled south & changed his style,
learning, it appears, a language moving
upon consequence, and consequently moved among
the circles of the powerful & into spaces
occupied by EICs and Nabobs. With a pamphlet
written for Mohamed Ali Chan, he scattered
all the nouveaux riches in London.

To my surprise,
I find I rather like him,
this child of the Macpherson clan
who came to be MP from Camelford and drive
a private coach, though it's true
I cannot read his book for very long.
Who can say what spoke to him
in Ruthven, tiny village on the Highland Road
near Perth where plowmen unearthed shards
of Roman bowls & where the farmers
scratched St Kattan's name as *Chattan*
on the Druid stones. Here he saw
an end that emptied the entire north
of ancient feeling. The broken clansmen
staggered to his very door. It was
the Highland Army's last assembly; Cluny had
a price upon his head; Macphersons fled,
then hid him; Charles was somewhere
in the islands or in France. The barracks

where Macpherson played a soldier burned,
and he was nine. Then enormous quiet.

I close the book and walk out on the shingle
staring into low wet fog upon the Firth
that rolls against the rocks like spindrift.
The beach is empty, save for one old man
and one black bird that's flying toward the mine.
The limbs of trees are heavy, drip—
as if with melting snow.

                            When old men faltered
in their songs
Macpherson squared the widening empty circles
with what came to hand: with rocks,
with fogs, with dripping trees, deserted beaches
and old men by which heraldic birds
were briefly lured to perch
on names like *Fingal, Oscar, Gaul*
as if on severed limbs upon a field of slaughter
the sight of which did not appal
the rock nearby or wood and water which afforded
the clear eye a rare and charming beauty
where the Erse Nation was not furious with Lord North.
Seeking to fill emptiness, Macpherson
marked its boundaries,
surveyed & gerrymandered sentimental space—

Samuel Johnson filled that space
with rage, Napoleon with a military will.
They too longed for grander feelings; an actual object
and a cause. Heraldic birds appeared
on the horizon, flying north.
Macpherson travelled south.
The Earl of Wemyss stared happily upon his Venus
signed *Van Dyck*.

IX

And I stare quizzically at what I've written here,
at language that has used me one more time
for consequential or inconsequential ends that
are not mine. Can I tell which (& where)
by making declarations: the one? the other, now?
By speaking Edward's language
to his dear and faithful cousin, Eymar de Valance,
as a second generation speaks
the ruins of a first?
                              by finding not
in our
Sir Michael Wemyss
good word? or occupying picturesque positions
on the summit of a cliff?

Can I tell which (& whose) by calling points
that mark the intersection of some arbitrary boundaries
castle, queen, and *mine?*
boundaries of a space by no means empty
where the cost of lodging
is exacted by a pile of books, by *castle, queen,* and *mine,*
attainted absent lord, and black heraldic bird?
I close the book and walk out on the shingle
staring into low wet fog, etcetera.
I never closed the book. I never left the room
to walk along the beach.

                              Tourist? Paying guest—
of language of
the place, but heading further north
and pledging silence.

I've heard a scholar filled his empty life
by tracing down a thousand plagiaries from eighty
sources in MacP. I've heard the casket letters
occupied a thousand scholars who had emptiness to fill
for half a thousand years. Otherwise,
who knows, they might have filled those spaces
with the motions of a Bothwell or a Cumberland

through whom the language of the place
spoke itself to consequence.

I've heard a man found Waverley "so colourless
and unconvincing as to be
a virtual
                    gap on the page."

And where are you, Kirkpatrick? (& Matthias)

Or you—
                    whose little ship ran battle-scarred
before the wind to Norway, piloted
by Hanseatic sailors well past lowland Karmoi.
Did you follow then the rocky coast to Bergen?
and from there a black heraldic bird
to Copenhagen, Malmö? Did you sail north from Orkney
shouting into gales, spoken for by oaths,
language howling you to silence deep as Dragsholm?
Did she say, whose French was not
Brantôme's, whose verse appalled Ronsard,
l'oiseau sortira de sa cage? And did she say, before
Kirkcaldy chased you through the mists
around the Orkneys, *Sonnets in italic hand*
conjure you to Scania. . . .
You'll crawl in squalid circles for eleven years & more
widdershins
and widdershins, weeping. . . .

So Bothwell's route is mine. I'll stuff my mouth
with herring, think of Anna Throndsen,
and not return to Fife either with the Maid of Norway
or the Duke of Orkney's head.
My bird of Sentiment took flight from Inverness.
Tangent to our Baltic steamer's course, he's plighted
to a Hanseatic taxidermist who will stuff him
for an øre—
                    Or: *l'oiseau sortira de sa cage?*

Old Bert Brecht, wily exile,
fleeing just ahead
of the Gestapo,
making for L.A. by way of Finland,

did you really see "High up in Lapland
towards the polar arctic sea,
a smallish hidden door"?

Through that door *black wings, yellow beak*
round eyes . . .

           appear a moment, pause

              & disappear

An East Anglian Diptych

in memoriam Robert Duncan and David Jones

Ley Lines

I

. . . & flint by salt by clay
by sunrise and by sunset
and at equinox, by equinox,

these routes, these
lines were drawn, are drawn,
(force by source of sun)

The dowser leans by Dod-man's
ley alignment and
against some oak by water now.

II

By flint: the tools
By salt: the meats
By clay: the rounded pots

Along the lines, by sun-
rise & by sunset
and at equinox, by equinox,

the Dod-man's sighting staves,
one in each hand, is it,
of that scoured long chalk man?

III

Past Tom Paine's house behind the puddingstone
and castle there aligned
strategically along the Icknield way

Beyond the Gallows Hill
beside the Thetford tracks to Brandon
down the Harling Drove

Across the Brickkiln Farm to Bromehill Cottage
& below the tumuli before
the rabbit warrens and top hats . . .

Some burials, some dead,
and here their flinted offerings.
Seven antler picks,

A phallus made of chalk,
a Venus (did they call her yet Epona?)
and a tallow lamp . . .

Beltane fire line forty miles long?
Conflagration's law where energy's electric
down the *herepath*

if *Belus* is spelt *Bel* . . .

•

No bronze until the Beakers.
No phosphorus lucifers until, say, 1832.
Toe holes, ropes allowed descent

for wall stone you could antler out,
shovel with a shoulder bone—
Floor stone you would crawl for . . .

Between the galleries, burrows
narrow as a birth canal, as dark,
where some half-blinded Neolith first

nudged the Brandon Blacks & passed
those flints as far down time as Waterloo.
Weapons, tools. Ornaments as well.

Flushwork on Long Melford Church.
Flint flake Galleting on Norfolk Guildhall.
Jags by thousands of the calcined stones

for Queen Victoria's potteries.
Strike-a-lights required on Maundy Thursday still—
oldest flints ignite a young god's Pascal wick,

But first an edge to cut away the underbrush
down ley lines
long before the Beakers and their bronze.

IV

Ten days, twelve chapters, and the young man soon to die at Arras finishes his book, his thirtieth or so, on the Icknield way. It's mostly about walking. He walks from Thetford where he thinks the Way begins coming from the Norfolk ports across the River Thet and Little Ouse. He's melancholy. The times are difficult, he's poor, he'd rather be a poet, his wife is desperate for his company, his children miss him too, a war is coming on, and, anyway, he's melancholy by nature. He has a friend who tries to show him how to turn his prose to verse. He'll have two years to do just that before he dies on Easter Monday, 1917.

But now he walks and writes. It is a job. They pay you for these nature books, these evocations, all this naming you can do along the road and through the villages and over all the dykes. They'll buy your eye even if they're deaf to all this balancing of consonants and vowels. He's melancholy. He doesn't really want to take this walk. He does it for the money. The times are difficult, he's poor, he'd rather be a poet, his wife is desperate for his company, his children miss him too, a war is coming on. Still,

It's better on a path than on a pavement.
It's better on the road than in a town.
It's better all alone to walk off melancholy
than to poison a companionable air
(or stare out of a muddy trench in France.)

Home, returned on leave, exhausted,
bored by prose he's published only months before
and talking with a friend who'll ask:
And what are you fighting for over there?

he'll pick a pinch of earth up off the path
they're walking and say: *This!*
For this, he'll say.
This This This

For

    this

       ●

This King Belinus was especially careful
to proclaim that cities
and the highways that led unto them

would have the peace
Dunwello had established in his time.
But no one seemed to know

the rules or lines whereby the boundaries
of the roads had been determined.
Neither Geoffrey, who, saying that about

Belinus in his book then consults the works
of Gildas, nor Gildas either,
nor Nennius himself in *Historia Brittonum.*

Before Belinus paved the road to "Hamo's Port"
with stone and mortar as he paved
Foss Way and Watling Street, walkers who

brought flint, brought salt, brought clay,
paved the way in footprints over peat
and grasses with their animals before them

or behind. *By flint:* the tools;
By salt: the meats; *by clay:* the rounded pots.
By ley lines, flint and clay and salt

by sunrise and by sunset
and at equinox, by equinox, these routes,
these lines were drawn

(but no one seemed to know the rules
whereby the boundaries
of the roads had been determined)

force by source of sun.

V

They leaned into the journey,
east to west,
beyond Grimes Graves and through

the place that would be Thetford.
For every dragon heard to have been slain,
they found a standing stone. . . .

Beside the Hill of Helith and then
along the river Lark
they left their weapons and their coins,

wondered at the headless rider
riding on the muddy banks. Cautious, curious
at the Swales tumulus, at

barrows north of Chippenham, they guessed
fine Wessex bronze lay gleaming
in the buried dagger there . . . and aged (grew young),

passed by Burwell church, passed by
Burwell castle too, spoke
of Anna and of Etheldreda, queen and saint,

at Exing, saw the horses race along
by Devil's Ditch to Reach, gallop through
the sainfoin which they gathered

in their hands as stone aligned with stone,
church with church, holy well
with holy well, pylon (in the end) with pylon.

Counting *one five four: four seven four:*
four eight six at Whittlesford,
brides among them turned their heads

to gaze at Golliwog, Shiela-na-gig.
Whose giggle, then, this
gog-eyed goggle goddess ogling back

above the portal near the Wandlebury
Gogmagog? *By air:* the zodiac;
By fire: the dragon path; *by earth:*

the tumulus, the barrow and the grave.
East to west
they leaned into the journey where

the dowser leans by Dod-man's
ley alignment and
against some oak by water now.

Rivers

I

By touch: his twig reveals the waters,
his sounding rod bites into chalk.
Matrona, Bel and Wandil gather in the mist

upon the hillside, lean into the journey:
moon by sun against the darkness,
sun by moon against the giant with a sword.

By air: the signal from the Gogmagogs
to zodiacs at Edmund's Bury and Nuthamstead.
Knight to knight come forth. By air

the still response: the bull, the lion;
the eagle & the bear. If Wandil stole the spring,
spread his frost along the ley lines,

now he strides as Gemini across the sky.
(Not two children, not two goats,
but eyes of Wandil rain down geminids

where ancient Dod-men lie. . . .)

II

By water now. Along the Lark to Bury
where by air the constellations
blaze down on these figures born of earth.

Was it before Beodricsworth became
Saint Edmund's town & shrine
that Sigebert's forebears paced off zodiacs

from Abbots Bridge to Stoke-by-Clare
discerned as fit propitiation still
by him who led the garlanded white bull

to its oblation for the barren girl
between imposing portals
of the Benedictine Abbey on the Lark?

By rivers then. Along this quiet one
past Bury where it forms
the tail of Sagittarius and on by sting

of Scorpio, by tribute and by tributary,
portaging on over Virgo
north of Shimpling to Chad Brook. . . .

Where the Stour flows by Long Melford
they leaned into their journey, rowed along
the belly of the Lion close by Clare.

If Wandil gestured to the west, they
travelled east toward Harwich, backs against
the morning sun, oars against the tide.

Underbrush along the banks at first
held only otters, then at Mysteleigh solemn men
sat fishing, men knelt making salt;

at Manningtree, a single lighter hauled
the heavy stones up shallow higher reaches
where a mason waited with his tools

and visions of a chancel in his brain.
Stoke and Wilford built their low stone bridges then;
other towns built locks; local wool

brought bricks and lime and coal.
West to east, they met the horse-drawn barges,
passed young woodsmen felling trees

to build the *Thorn,* the *Syren* and the *Terpsichore.*
Lark by Stour by Orwell; Scorpio
by Lion. Moon by sun against the darkness.

Sun by moon. A giant with a sword. . . .

III

Or with a ship. A *Syren* or a *Terpsichore.* And if a giant, then a giant metamorphosed
over time. The man who'll six years later paint the *Hay Wain* may not know his river
rises as a tiny brook east of the Chilterns in the Gogmagogs. And yet he feels the giant
in it, yet he knows its gods. Today he finishes his sketch of Flatford Mill—the mill
itself, the locks, the barge and bargemen, and the small distracted barefoot boy on his
horse. He'll work it up in 1817 for the Academy and no one will complain that it lacks
finish. The sketch itself is rough. He adds an ash—his favorite tree—some elms, a
broken oak. He shades in clouds he's come to study with a meteorologist's precision.
Then he shuts the sketch book and trudges off toward Dedham, marking in his mind
the river's fringe of willowherb and reed, the rising heron and the darting snipe and
redshank in the sky . . .

He wants to marry Charles Bicknell's daughter. He wants to paint this river and these
shimmering green fields. He doesn't want to quarrel with Charles Bicknell, with the
rector of his village, or with Bonaparte. And he doesn't want to paint for money por-
traits of the rich or of their homes: Malvern Hall, Petworth House, East Bergholt.
The ships that followed *Thorn* on down the slips at Mistly shipyards belched a thou-
sand years of Beltane fire at French sails on the Nile. Martello towers rose at Shotley
and at Walton Ferry . . . But here and now it's quiet, he thinks. Here and now it's
peaceful and the air is pure . . .

It's better to paint rivers than great houses.
It's better to be married than alone.
It's better with companionship to sit through winter nights
remembering the Stour in springtime
(or a cousin lying face-down in the mud at Waterloo).

Here, returned from London, nervous and annoyed,
bored by portraits that he's painted only months before
and talking to a friend who asks:
And what are you drawing landscapes for out here?

he picks a pinch of earth up off the path
they're walking and says *This!*
For this, he says.
This This This
For

        this

       •

This other ryver called of old time
Fromus maketh his beginning
near to Framlingham and then descendeth

close by Marlesford and so
southeast of Farnham entertayneth yet
another ryver called the Gleme

which cometh out from Rendlesham
thus passing forth to Snapebridge and
contriving then his course to Yken

dedicates himself into the sea
not very far away from where the Stour & Orwell
run together into Harwich harbour.

Framlingham: Framela's people: strangers on
the Fromus before Fromus became Alde.
Folk who'd become burgen-holders paying 5d tax.

On the bluff above the mere the Bigods' castle
glowers: Henry's castle glowers back
from Orford. Herrings, cereals, pottery from

Staverton passed through the town, began a journey
inland or a journey to the coast.
Scratchings on the nave in Parham church

show navigable reaches: ships of little draft
came all the way from Normandy past
Orford, Sloughden, Iken, down this stream

that flows
into a pipe below a petrol station

now

IV

. . . Men will number
what they value most
in wills: 'To Robert Cook my scalbote,

my anchor and the things belonging to it and
my spurling bote: to George Clare
my fysher, fartle, makerel nets & warropes:

To John Weylonde: A manfare of haryngnetts:
capstaynes, skewers & my sparlyng netts
that hangeth in the low to the sea this yere

and when the sparlyngfare is done the netts
schal then be partyd to my children:
Thomas, Christopher, Erasmus: ships belonging

to the havyn to be sold at Aldeburgh church.'
The men who made the wills were fishermen;
The others built their boats along these shores . . .

or sold them victuals, or worked upon the land,
or herded sheep, kept inns, cut
the timber, prayed in church & monastery, wept

impressed at sea, took up piracy and smuggling,
made the malt that made the ale they drank,
organized themselves in unions, and were hanged.

By 1850 photographs appear to show us
what they looked like outside Newton Garrett's
maltings or beside their barges loading

at Snape quay. John Felgate, shipwright, has
no teeth and wears a cap of moleskins;
his son, standing by a dinghy, has a thick

mustache, a threadbare coat, & a determined gaze.
Jack Ward, skipper of the *Gladys,* smiles;
his heavy begrimed turtleneck presses up against

his graying whiskers and his wide square chin.
The carpenters, Alfred Andrews & his son,
look almost well-to-do beside the shipwrights;

the younger Andrews wears a tie, a waistcoat,
and a golden chain while sawing timber for a rudder
or a boom; Howell and Chatten, maltsters,

hold their massive wooden shovels, handles down,
and slop about in canvas boots. Their rugged faces
look like copper pennies in a winter sun.

If we could hear them speak we'd doubtless hear
them say how *chance-times a sloe-wind*
brings old Tabbler Cable back to that same mawther

who'd 'im clapper-clawed or hear them laugh about
the crones who *couldn't sculpt the roots*
out as they got no teeth. The carter thakketh his hors

upon the croupe and jumps up in his wagon.
He's off to town. The men who work the maltings
and the bargemen line up for their pay.

The bird that flies about them angling toward
the Orford Ness they call a *mavis;*
by the time it reaches sprawling spider-webs

of early-warning radar nets it's lost its name,
and anyone at Chantry Point
looking with binoculars for avocets or curlews

would only see, if it passed by, a thrush.
Along the ley-alignment point
at Sizewell, Beltane fires in the reactor

are contained by water drained out of the sea.

V

     . . . But that the salt sea of say AD 500
should be drained from Deben marshes
that the land be sweet for corn and cattle . . .

That the river rising beyond Sutton, beyond
Woodbridge wait out flood & tide
for Norman engineers and then the Dutch,

for every local Fosdike, every local Waller
who might learn the warping
and the inning, reclaim with bank & seawall

or with sluice & gutter marshes then defended
by the reeves of Walton and
the men of Melton who might write: *lately salt,*

now fresh . . . That would take some time.
Some time, too, before the signals flash from
castle cresset, lucomb, lighthouse

or Martello tower up and down the coast
from Goseford to the Alde. No
early warnings here where everything's surprise.

South to north, they leaned into the journey,
rounded Landguard Point and
passed by Walton Castle, sailing with the tide

across the sand bar, steersman hugging
his athwartship tiller, small rain
in the oarsmen's eyes, wind across the stern.

Beyond the sandy heathland, the turf & bracken
over which they'd lug a ship the
size of this one to be buried as a cenotaph—

with coins from Usson-du-Poitou, a golden helmet,
maple lyre, & stone sceptre carved
with eight stern faces and a thin bronze stag

mounted on its delicate iron ring—
they reached the pools they sought and, anchoring
off mud flats, felled the trees,

built their timber halls beyond abandoned villas,
stayed at Hemley, Hatchley, Trimley,
called the river that they sailed "the deep one."

They'd say they lived in *Middanyeard,* where *haeleth
under heofenum:* they found themselves
between two seas . . . (the hero of their poem the sun).

Before them, Celts and Roman legions.
After them the Viking raids.
After them the Norman engineers and Flemish traders.

Before them, the single salters squatting
on the mud, the long walk for flints
along the Icknield way. After them the excavation

of the buried ship. . . .

●

Extensio. Eastern point
north of Southwold on the Easton Ness, now lost.
Portus Adurni. Was the Deben called Adurnus

by the Latins here and on the Alde?
Harbour, temperate climate, sheltered creeks—
and vines growing high above the cliffs.

Counts of the Saxon Shore constructed here
their fortress where they failed to hold the tide
against the kin of those first called

by Vortigern to fight his wars against the Picts.
(St. Alban's first cartographer
would clearly mark his map: *Angulus Anglie* . . .)

Around the corner, then, and up the river
with the driftwood & the tide. Buoyed and beaconed,
spits and banks first marked with small

bouquets of yellow broom display their
angled emblems: Bowships beacon, Middleground,
Upper Waldringfield and Lower Ham,

Jack Rush beacon, Crimmy Moore, Horse Buoy.
If Edward were to anchor here
along the Kingsfleet, who but the Archbishop

might come sailing smartly out of Shotley
as the king, shining like some Helith, went to meet him
round into the Stour? On board the *Thomas,*

in a western wind, the Goseford ships impressed
for service, the power upon them
& Calais in fear, they'd break up the Great Seal.

So Wandil on the Stour gestures gravely
to the Wandil on the Gogmagogs. Against him lean
the sun & moon while all about him

widdershins there turns a circle of the dancers
who will help achieve the spring
as every ley south-east of Thetford Castle Mound

lines up along the tumuli and standing stones
to pass through places named for Bel
or Belus out to Walton on the northern Sea. . . .

Beyond the Roman camp, the Saxon mound.
Beyond the Saxon mound the Viking
outpost in the Celtic forest with its secret paths.

Along the paths, the route to tributaries,
creeks, the sweetest hidden wells. Above the wells
a dowser with his twig, a Dod-man

with his sighting staves. . . .

•

who walks along the concrete wall,
and feels the fresh salt air,
and watches small yachts ply the quiet river

at high tide. Red sails, blue.
And bright white hulls. Woodbridge Sunday sailors
tack and jibe . . .

Alde by Stour by Deben. Ship by Saxon shore.
Cattle, corn by sea wall.
Dod-man, dowser, dapple of reflected cloud.

Facts from an Apocryphal Midwest

For Ken Smith and Michael Anania

I. Seven Moves Toward Embarkation on the Local River

Nous embarquâmes le troisième Decembre
avec trente hommes, dans huit canots

& nous remontâmes la rivière des Miamis
faisant nostre route au Sud . . .

—Fr. Hennepin

•

Overheard on Riverside cycling toward
the bridge and U.S. 31:
Look, he says, *if things had turned out*

differently a long time back,
not just you, but everybody on this
river might be speaking French

& trading otter skins or beaver pelts.

•

1 arpent: 160 *pieds de Roi*
84 arpents: say about one league
28 arpents, then, to the mile

But distances are tricky
and it often takes
you longer
than you think.

•

Four thin men, two white, two black
stand fishing near the Farmer's Market
where the Amish come to sell

their vegetables and breads. It's early
afternoon in heavy, muggy August.
The river's low & stagnant for ten miles.

Catchin' anything? Jus' tin cans an' tires
Four thin fishermen—
and no Miamis, not a Potawatomi in town.

•

Oui-oui-la-Meche
L'Espérance de la Brie

Père Gabriel
Père Louis
Père Zénobe

Réné Robert Cavelier (Sieur de la Salle)

•

"There were several varieties of league; but the one that Hennepin undoubtedly meant was the ordinary league of 84 arpents. That will give 3.051 plus 5220-5280th statute miles. You need have no hesitation in assuming Hennepin's league to be 3.052 statute or English miles."

"We embarked on the 3rd of December with thirty men in eight canoes, and ascended the river of the Miamis, taking our course to the south-east for about twenty five leagues. We could not make out the portage which we were to take with our canoes and all our equipage in order to go and embark at the source of the river Seignelay, and as we had gone higher up in a canoe without discovering the place where we were to march by land to take the other river which runs by the Illinois, we halted to wait for the Sieur de La Salle, who had gone exploring on land; and as he did not return we did not know what course to pursue."

—Fr. Hennepin

2. Five Maps, a Medicine Bag, and a Myth

•

Carte de la Nouvelle Découverte

Illuminations of the priests haranguing Indians.
Much conjecture. Crudely drawn Ohio
and Missouri and Wisconsin . . .
Père Marquette's route back it's got
entirely wrong.

•

Carte Générale de la France Septentrionale

The Ohio's called the *Ouaboustikou.*
Pictures of the creatures
native to the Mississippi's western plains
include a camel, ostriches, giraffes.
A monster seen by Père Marquette and Joliet:
Horns of a deer, beard of a tiger,
face like that of a man—Also
many nasty scales
and a long tail wound around it.

•

Carte de Jean Baptiste Franquelin

La Salle's Starved Rock, a natural fortress
all but inaccessible a hundred feet
above the Illinois, the little colony below.
La Nouvelle France: Penobscot
to the south of Lake Champlain and to
the Mohawk near Schenectady
and then where Susquehanna rises
and the Allegheny past the south of Erie
on to Southern Michigan & then
northwest to Mississippi tributaries.
La Louisiane: The Mississippi valley,

the Ohio valley, Texas.
Rivière Colbert. Grande Rivière des Emissourittes.
Rivière des Illinois, ou Macopins.
And down below Starved Rock the colony:
Shawnees, Ouiatenons, Miamis,
Piankishaws, Illinois, Kilaticas, & Ouabonas.
3,900 warriors huddling
under *Le Rocher* & trembling for the Iroquois.

●

Carte de M. Mathieu Sâgean

The nation of the Acanibas, towns and castles,
King Hagaren, Montezuma's kin.
Women riding unicorns. Bricks of solid gold.
Caravans of horsemen
and a thousand oxen bearing priceless treasures.
Everyone polygamist.
Perpetual summer there, a cool breeze.

●

Rand McNally Atlas, 1985

The old Sauk trail, they say
still runs under U.S. 12
north from Niles to Detroit.
U.S. 20 takes it west through
Rolling Prairie to Chicago.

You can drive a car that's named
for Cadillac up U.S. 12
to Ypsilanti, turning north
at 94 to a port named for the Hurons.
You can even drive
your Pontiac to Pontiac.
But only trickster Wiske's brother
Chibyabos ever drove
in a Tecumseh to Tecumseh.

●

What's in your medicine bag, Neshnabe?
Gifts from Wiske? Toys?

A skunk's bladder. Ear of a bat.
Three fat joints and a switchblade knife.
Pussy hairs from Mama Chickie's whores.
What's in your map, little Frog?
If I drop this at your feet, it will explode.

•

The story goes that poor and feeble Tisha had a vision. A stranger dressed elaborately in clothing he had never seen before appeared and said he'd build a boat for him to travel over land and sea and rivers in if Tisha showed him just how big it ought to be. Tisha then took twelve enormous paces, smiled at the solemn stranger, waited. Suddenly a ship appeared the likes of which he'd never seen or even dreamed of. It had thin tree trunks planted vertically upon its decks, it had white sheets attached, it had nine great guns. Boat-Maker and Tisha climbed aboard and sailed over land and sea and rivers. They met and took aboard a mighty seer, a mighty hearer, a mighty eater, a mighty runner, and a mighty maker of wind. These were Boat-Maker's friends.

One day after many travels they arrived at the camp of evil Matjimanito. He and all his friends were cannibals, and many bones lay all around. Matjimanito challenged Tisha to a contest where he'd gamble for his life. When Boat-Maker saw poor Tisha trembling, he insisted on a game which Matjimanito had never played before. When Tisha shouted *now,* Wind-Maker blew the ship up in the air above the village shouting out: *everybody's bones get out of here!* The nine black cannons fired, the dead all came alive, and Matjimanito and his men all perished when the ship came down and crushed them. After that, Tisha was a famous man. He travelled all the world over with his elegant protector and his friend. Eventually, Boat-Maker taught him how to speak his language. It was French.

3. Copper. South from Lake Superior

. . . and down the old Sauk trail
although there were then, three and more millennia
before the French, no Sauks. . . .

The trail itself was there, and those who mined
the copper, *they* were there,
and those who came on urgent journeys from

the lower Mississippi & the Gulf to lug it back
were there, and leaned into
their labors in the mines and on the paths.

Mounds at Moorhouse Parish, at Miamisburg,
tumuli along the northeast
of the marshy lake between the Kankakee and

Portage Prairie with its recent graves & glacial
memories of mastodon & mammoth spit up
needles, chisels, knives & awls in fine profusion—

& when Bernal Diaz entered Tuspan with Cortez,
he found that *every Indian had,*
besides his ornaments of gold, a copper axe,

very highly polished, strangely carved.
The copper came from west and north
of Mackinaw, Sault Ste. Marie, & Whitefish point.

from Minong where ten thousand men once mined
the copper for a thousand years
but left no carvings, writings, signs, nothing

but their simple tools. Their dead they
buried elsewhere. Jacques Marquette was first to put
the island on a white man's map. . . .

If the copper came by water to the forest paths,
it came by long canoe along the shores
of Huron into Lake St. Clair and then Detroit

where the trail curved into Canada.
Was Father Claude Allouez, the Jesuit, correct
who said of them who called

themselves *Neshnabek* and the other
tall Algonquins at Green Bay that golden copper
shapes were manitous, that queerly

wrought and efficacious metals were the secret
household gods of Potawatomies
who worshipped, like grave alchemists, the sun?

4. Saint-Lusson, Green Bay

The King of all these Frenchmen *was* the sun,
or so he liked to say, and Saint-
Lusson's vain oratory blazed with a brightness

at Green Bay outshining any local *kiktowenene's.*
But did he know to whom he spoke? Did
he know the phratries and the clans? Who was Bear

and who was Wolf or Bird, Elk or Moose or Fox?
He knew less of them than they knew
of the ones who built the mounds and made the trails

and mined the copper glowing in their lodges.
Chaskyd the ventriloquist? Wabino
eating fire? What was sleight of hand & superstition

to these soldiers of the King who sang *Vexilla Regis*
and the Jesuits who dreamed theocracy
and sought to make of these great lakes a Paraguay?

Nicholas Perrot, himself a spirit-power
said every Shaman there, assembled lines of Winnebagoes,
Potawatomies, Menomonies and Sauks before the *engagés,*

and cynical *coureurs de bois,* before the priests, before
the silken Saint-Lusson. *Vive Le Roi,* he said,
picking up a clod of earth and brandishing his sword. . . .

Did Wiske smile on these transactions, throw
tobacco on the fire? And did his brother Chibyabos chant
beyond the sunset names that sounded there

like Onangizes and Onontio? *Vive Le Roi, and hail*
the highest and most mighty monarch and
most Christian King of France and of Navarre

for whom I take possession of this place Sault St. Marie
and also lakes Superior and Huron also
Manitoulin also all the countries rivers lakes and

streams contiguous adjacent thereunto both those dis-
covered and the ones we will discover
in their length & breadth & bounded only by the seas

declaring to the nations living there that they
from this time forth are vassals
of his Majesty bound by laws & customs which are his.

Then Allouez harangued them about Jesus.
Francis Parkman writes: "What remains of sovereignty
thus pompously proclaimed?

Now and then
the accents of some straggling boatman or
a half-breed vagabond—

this and nothing more."

5. Making of the Rivers and the Prairies

Before that rhetoric, that epigraph,
gushing of the ancient, unheard waters all along
the terminal moraine. Before the melt,

Maumee ice flow inching toward a Wabash
where no water ran, a Saginaw
into a dry Dowagiac. Before an unbound Kankakee,

glacial borders pressing ice lobes out
to flood the valley where no valley was, to spread
the drift two hundred feet and more above

Coniferous, Devonian and Trenton rock.
Before the flood, copper manitous locked up in stone
on distant islands not enisled

before the miners who would dig for them
where no mines were and build the pregnant mounds
by forest trails that were not blazed.

Before the forest trails, before the oak & ash,
path of the moraine: sand & boulders,
quartzite, clay and till . . .

Before the Potawatomies. Before the French.
Before the Studebaker &
the Bendix and the Burger Chef. . . .

●

10,000 years ago
the Erie ice, the Saginaw,
the Michigan converged just here.

Hills and ranges fixed the contours then.
Basins formed, and runoff made
two rivers wider than the Mississippi.

Tributaries broke through lateral moraines.
The Elkhart and the Yellow rivers
drained away the last of Maumee glacier—

no waters yet could run off to Desplaines.
When they did, the two great rivers
slowed—silted up their valleys with debris

and changed their names.
Turning on itself, Dowagiac became its former
tributary, flowing to Lake Michigan.

Kankakee at flood time
emptied into the immense abandoned channel,
flowed on to St. Joseph, left

an ice gorge, then a sand bar and a bluff
here at Crum's Point.
Drainage opened to the east

all the way beyond the lakes to the St. Lawrence.
Water levels fell, channels
slowly narrowed, and the River of Miamis

took its present course. Curving to the south.
Flowing to the north.
Rising where it fell in the beginning.

So Crum's Point burst its ice-dam and
the Kankakee flowed mostly with the stronger
new and narrow river now.

Silted up to fourteen feet, the site
of a confluence sealed itself with rock
and sand and soil: made

a watershed on the continental divide.
Above, the level sand plain. And below, the marsh:
Seignelay south-west, & Illinois.

From a millennium of glacial drift, the prairies
now had formed: Portage, Palmer
Sumption . . .

       Terre Coupée. . . .

      •

      But on these waters:
Could you sail a ship?
And on this land: *Found an empire now*

surrounded on the north and east by oak & hickory? On the south adjoining: scat-
tered clumps of alders, willow bushes native to these soils. The prairie reached from portage
landing two and one half miles, three & more from the nearest eastern verge. To the west
& south, the vast expanse of grass and marsh appeared as one great plain. Deep into the
west, a stretch of rolling timber. . . .

6. The Boat-Maker's Tale

He'd sent the Griffin on back to Niagara
loaded with the furs he thought
would play his debts. . . .
      Colbert walked in shadows

at Versailles, the river to be named for him
named otherwise by Onangizes, called
himself, like Colbert's king, the shimmering sun.

Frontenac, Onnontio to Green Bay's Ouilamette
and all the rest of Gigos clan,
dreamed a map of colonies and little forts

stretching from above St. Joseph on the lake
down the river of Miamis
to the marshy waters of that languid

tributary to be named one day for Seignelay
whose own necrology of ships
made him Minister among the idle admirals

in the shipyards and the ports of France.
Stretching farther still . . .
Stretching well beyond that river to the one

that only Joliet and Père Marquette
among the French had ever seen & named & spoken of
saying that *no land at all no*

country would be better suited to produce
whatever fruits or wheat or corn
than that along this river that the wild cattle

never flee that one finds some 400 in a herd
that elk & deer are almost every-
where and turkeys promenade on every side. . . .

From the day a man first settled here
that man
could start to plow. . . .
                              But Cavelier, La Salle,

had sent the Griffin on back to Niagara.
He'd build a second ship
to sail down the rivers he would find. . . .

For he himself had said in Paris, sounding
just like Père Marquette, *it's all
so beautiful and fertile, free from forests*

*full of meadows brooks and rivers all
abounding there in fish & game
where flocks and herds can even be left out*

all winter long. All winter long!
And it was nearly winter now in Michillimackinak.
The King had said to him *We have received*

*with favor a petition in your name and do
permit your exploration
by these presents signed with our own hand*

but now he was in debt. Migeon, Charon—
they'd seized the beaver pelts
and even skins of skunks—Giton, Pelonquin!

Names of enemies. But there was Henri Tonty here;
there was, indeed, Count Frontenac.
These he'd name against the plotting creditors.

The ship will fly above the crows, he'd said,
his patron governor's heraldic mast-
head besting Jesuits in a Niagaran dream of power.

He had his Récollets to do whatever of God's work
there was. Hennepin, who strapped
an altar on his back and cured the fainting

Father Gabriel with a confection of hyacinths!
and Gabriel himself; and Zénobe.
They'd sung *Te Deum* well enough upon the launching.

He'd have them sing a good deal more than that—
Exaudiat, Ludovicus Magnus!—
once they'd reached the Colbert's mouth, the sea.

The ship *had* nearly flown across the lakes.
In spite of an ungodly pilot
and in spite of god knows dreadful storms

she'd been the equal of the Erie and the Huron.
How she'd sailed out beyond Niagara!
Her canvas billowed & she fired her five small guns

to the astonishment of Iroquois along the banks.
Then a freshening northwest wind.
Down the lake and to Detroit's narrow straights

she sailed until she met a current there strong
as the bore before the lower Seine—
and twelve men leapt ashore to pull her over, through.

They marvelled at the prairies to the east & west
and stopped to hunt, and hung their
guyropes full of fowl and drying bearskins.

From wild grapes the priests prepared communion wine.
Then they were in Huron where the gale
attacked them and they brought down mainyards, tacked

with trysail, then lay long to the till.
The pilot blasphemed damnably while all the rest
cried out to Anthony of Padua

who calmed the winds and brought the ship to port
at Michillimackinak beside
the mission of St. Ignace, Père Marquette's fresh grave.

That was in the early autumn when the Ottawa
and Huron fishing fleets
were strung across the lakes from Saint Marie du Sault

to Keweenwa, from Mackinac to Onangizes' islands
in Green Bay. He'd worn his scarlet coat
with its gold lace and flown the banner of the king

while all his men fired muskets & he stepped ashore.
That was autumn, when the sun
still burned their necks & missionaries harvested.

But it was nearly winter now and he would be he said
in Illinois country when the rivers froze.
Heavy clouds blew in from Canada on northern winds.

The ship had sailed away. And so they
set forth on the lake in four canoes: fourteen men
who bore with them a forge & carpenters' &

sawyers' tools to build the Griffin's twin
beside a fort they'd also build on high ground near
the navigable lower Illinois.

They cried out to each other in the dark.
For it was dark before they were across the lake.
It stormed again as when the Griffin

rocked and shook on Huron, waves against the fragile
birchbark, rain in their red eyes.
Anvil and bellows, iron for nails and bolts,

pit-saws, arms, and merchandise for gifts
and trade when they had reached the Illinois town below
the portage weighed them down.

Gunsmith, blacksmith, joiner, mason, master-
builder Moyse Hillère—
they paddled for the further shore with Cavelier

and three priests and the guide. Half of them
were cousins to *coureurs de bois*
and would desert. Two of them were felons.

All of them washed up together with the breaking
waves beside
the mouth of the Miamis

        and gorged on grapes and wild haws & on the carcass of a deer that
had been killed by wolves.

Here they stayed for twenty days, and built a tiny fort, and spiked the hill they built it on.
They took nine soundings of the river's mouth, marking out the passage that a ship might
take with buoys and bearskin flags. The first brief snow blew in across the lake well before
December and ice began to form along the river's edge. Occasionally, La Salle's Mohegan
guide could find a deer to kill, or bear, and brought them meat; but food was scarce and all
of them began to urge La Salle to press on to the portage and to Illinois or Miami camps
where they might find, in covered pits, a gleaming hoard of winter's corn. When Tonty fi-

nally came with men who had been sent ahead from Fort Niagara but had scattered in the woods, the party numbered thirty-four. Four were left behind with messages and maps for those who would arrive to reinforce them when the Griffin sailed back past Michillimackinak and down Lake Michigan & anchored here. If the Griffin wasn't lost. If the furs to pay off creditors had not been stolen by the pilot and his men. If all of them had not sailed straight to join the outlaw trader Dan Du Lhut at Kamalastigouia up in Thunder Bay.

Nous embarquâmes, wrote Hennepin, *le troisième Decembre. Avec trente hommes . . . Dans huit canots.* They were John Boisrondet, L'Espérance de la Brie, La Rousselière, La Violette, Picard du Gay, Etienne Renault, Michel Baribault, Bois d'Ardeene, Martin Chartier, Noel le Blanc, the nailer called La Forge, the Indian guide they called Oui-Oui-La-Meche, and those with names now known to all or names now known to none. They took up paddles once again, prepared to travel on, to shoulder their canoes along the portage trail if they could find it. Had it been spring, had it been high summer, the fields and woods that lined the river's channel would have blossomed for them, fruited like the prairies on the east and west of the Detroit straights when they pulled the Griffin through to Huron and the priests made wine. And when at last they reached the portage, they would have seen tall cedars, oaks, and water-elms; in a ravine declining from high ground they would have seen along the curving trail splashes of the reds and blues of wild forest flowers; flocks of plovers, snipe, might have flown above the trees to land beside the standing cranes in fields of wild rice in fens the far side of the watershed across the prairie with its elk and deer and buffalo which traders would begin to call one day the *Parc aux Vaches.* But it was winter; they saw none of this. They saw the skulls and bones of animals, a bleak gray plain; they lugged their eight canoes and forge and iron and anvil up the hill and then along the portage path behind La Salle who brooded on the Griffin in the melancholy, willful, isolated silence of his mind, La Salle whose men, with five exceptions, would forsake his vision and his surrogate at Fort Crevecoeur—39 degrees and 50 minutes latitude exactly on his fine Parisian astrolabe—and daub in tar-black letters on the planking of the half-built river boat: *Nous Sommes Tous Sauvages.*

The man who followed him in many ways was like him, and read his words, and read the words and followed all the trails of others who had passed this way before he did himself, but after him who was the first to come and was the object of his search. Charlevoix he read, and La Hontan. Tonty's own account, and Hennepin's, and all of La Salle's letters both to Canada and France. Transcripts, depositions. He too knew about insatiable ambition, pride and isolation, subduing all to an inflexibility of purpose. When his chronic and mysterious illness made his head swim and his joints swell, made his eyes so sensitive to light he could not read, his nights so sleepless that he could not even dream his shattered double's thousand mile trek from the lower Illinois back to Montreal, he had his friends read *to* him, tried to comprehend their strange pronunciations of the language of the texts and maps and manuscripts *de la France Septentrionale* which he followed to the Kankakee or Seignelay and then beyond. . . .

Terres tremblantes, sur lesquelles on peut à peine marcher he read, and wrote how "soon they reached a spot where oozy saturated soil quaked beneath their tread. All around were clumps of alder-bushes . . . pools of glistening water *une espèce de mare* and in the midst a dark and lazy current, which a tall man might bestride . . . twisting like a snake among the reeds and rushes and . . . *il a faut continuellement tourner* . . . They set canoes upon this thread of water and embarked their baggage and themselves and pushed on down the sluggish streamlet looking at a little distance like men who sail on land . . . Fed by an increasing tribute of the spongy soil it widened to a river *presque aussi large que la Marne,* and they floated on their way into a voiceless, lifeless solitude of boundless marshes overgrown with reeds. . . .

At night they built their fire on ground made firm by frost
quelques mottes de terres glacées

and bivouacked among rushes . . ."

7. Convergence . . . & Dispersion

Behind La Salle, before his blinking chronicler,
these others came. They came
to undo all designs of Tisha and his friends,

all designs conceived by Jesuit or Récollet
or empire builder in Quebec
or dreamed beneath Starved Rock among the Illinois.

These others came on urgent journeys of unmaking
and from very far away
but very fast and very quietly and no one knew.

They travelled not so much by river routes & streams
as by the trails. They came
because the French and their Algonquin allies

were establishing an iron monopoly
on furs which handsome ladies like Madame d'Outrelaise
and Madame Frontenac—*les divines*

they called them at Versailles—liked to drape around
their pink & chilly shoulders
when in Paris they would hear, at Arsanal,

the private recitations of Racine and Molière
or walk the Louvre along Perrault's
great colonnade, or walk le Brun's new gallery nearby.

These others walked the narrow trails
from Mohawk lodges on through busy Onondaga country
to the Senecan frontier—

These others were the Iroquois.
And when LaSalle objectively took note of 1680's comet
wondered at in Paris and the calculated

object of Sir Isaac Newton's will,
Increase Mather wrote upon the theocratic tablet of his soul:
A Portent! Well, it may have been.

Trade among the openings of oak and on the open prairie
would be anything but free.
And so they leaned into their journey, east to west,

and put a price upon it.
Over trails between the rivers flowing to the lakes
& those that flowed into the Susquehanna south—

then across the Seneca & north beyond Cayuga
to the watershed between Ontario and Erie, to Niagara.
Canadasegy, Canadaragey, Canawagus—

villages on ley lines into which their dancing feet
trod magic from the Hudson river west
and to Detroit. . . .

⦁

                              Behind the Iroquois,
the English and the Dutch.
Behind the Dutch and English, the Americans.

Braddock, Washington. Clark & Wayne & Harrison.
The Iroquois trails and the Sauk
widened to accommodate the marching of militias—

For convergence of new peoples in procession
down new roads, dispersion's
an express condition, and diaspora's required. . . .

Pontiac's conspiracy. Tecumseh's genius
and the wild hallucinations of the Shawnee prophet
in his Prophetstown. Black Hawk for an hour.

All the rest is trade—wagons made
by Clem and Henry Studebaker in a town Coquillard
founded for the Astors.

Oh, and Cooper's wooden Indians.
Standing near the banks of local rivers in his book
of 1848, they decorate a prairie

modelled now on European parks mown by gardeners
who themselves become like trees
on the green & flowering stage which they prepare

a decade after the removal of the Potawatomis.
They stand there like Pokagon, last
okama of the lakes whose little band did not accept

the Treaty of Chicago engineered by Billy Caldwell
but remained in his protection
and in his most pious Christian prayers, and even

in his fiction ghosted by a local lawyer's wife
whose husband pressed his claims
in every court. Cooper's stagecoach, meanwhile,

clatters past the Walker Tavern on the old Sauk trail
that's become the route of Western's
bright red buckboards & their Concord Coaches from Detroit.

The aging author whose new book will be dismissed
for tedious didacticism & a meager plot
engages Mrs. Martineau from London in a civil conversation

interrupted by her not infrequent jottings in a diary
about how wisely planned
and prettily she finds this road from Niles

which the Iroquois took to slaughter Illinois women
at Starved Rock and which, from
Ypsilanti down to Edwardsburg and then beyond

80,000 western emigrants began to stream by 1838 or 39.
We cross St. Joseph's River,
Mrs. Martineau observes, *upon a ferry towed by ropes.*

And as the clever horses pull us up the bank
we find ourselves in Indiana territory. She glances up
at Cooper who, in turn, acknowledges her smile.

The stagecoach travels on. Arriving from Fort Wayne,
and heading north & west along
what still they call the Dragoon Trail, the U.S. mail . . .

while ahead of it, turning just in front of Cooper's
coach on Michigan, honking Studebakers
and the children marching smartly off in little groups

before the dignitaries—councilmen & mayor
& some Elks & Shriners dressed to look like Potawatomi
and Illinois elders—

and everybody smiling at the camera
as if this were
some kind of local pageant

●

  & they gathered near the portage trail
to commemorate La Salle in a depression.
Hoover, says the Mayor, will employ honest citizens

to build a great historic monument. A corner
stone is laid. Massed bands of high school students play,
choirs singing in the cold . . . *Semper Fidelis.*

December 5, 1679. *Queleques mottes de terres glacées.*
Eight years later and
La Salle was murdered by conspirators in Texas.

A bell tower rises, in a man's imagination,
some two hundred feet. (The monument was never built.)
On the river, down below the pageant,

in a man's imagination or before him on his page
Now and then
the accents of a straggling boatman

or a half-breed vagabond
this &
nothing more . . .

A Compostela Diptych

For John Peck and Guy Davenport

Part I: France

I

Via Tolosona, Via Podiensis.
There among the tall and narrow cypresses,
the white sarcophagi of Arles

worn by centuries of wind & sun,
where Charlemagne's lieutenants it was said
lay beside Servilius & Flavius

and coffins drifted down the Rhone
on narrow rafts to be unloaded by St. Victor's monks,
they walked: Via Tolosona.

Via Podiensis: They walked as well from
Burgundy through the Auvergne,
slogged along volcanic downland up into Aubrac

and on through Languedoc to Conques
and gazed into the yellow morning light falling
from above the central axis through

the abbey's lantern tower
and praised St. Foy, and praised as well
with Aimery Picaud their guide

the names of certain travelers
who had long before secured the safety of their way
and also other ways: Via Podiensis,

Via Lemosina, Via Turonensis.
They crossed the Loire at Tours and at Nevers,
walking toward Bordeaux or

from St. Leonard and St. Martial of Limoges
to Périgord and to Chalosse.
At Tours beside the sandy, wide & braided river

they would rest a while and bathe
or seek the narrow shoals nearby & shallow streams
that ran between. Here St. Martin's

shrine had outfaced Abd-al-Rahman
and they prayed at his basilica remembering
the ninety thousand Moors

beaten back to Córdoba before Almansor
took the bells of Santiago
for his candle-sticks, hung them highly

in his elegant great mosque & upside down.
His singers sang of it.
These walking also sang: Via Lemosina,

Via Turonensis: they sang the way along the ways.
They sang the king: *Charles li reis,*
ad estet en Espaigne . . . *Tresqu'en la mer*

conquiste la terre altaigne. Trouvères, jongleurs,
langue d'oïl, lanque d'oc: of love
& war, the Matamoros & the concubine at Maubergeon.

And there was other song—song sung inwardly
to a percussion of the jangling
manacles and fetters hanging on the branded

heretics who crawled the roads
on hands and knees and slept with lepers under
dark facades of abbeys

& the west portals of cathedrals with their zodiacs.
These also sang: as had
the stern young men, their sheep or cattle

following behind, when up
to high summer pasture they would carry
from the scoria-red waste

a wooden image of their black and chthonic mother
burned in her ascent up out of
smoking Puy-de-Dome (or her descent

from very heaven: Polestar's daughter urging
them to Finisterre. . . .
                              Whichever way

they came they sang.
Whatever song they sang they came.
Whichever way they came, whatever song they sang,

they sang and walked together on the
common roads: Via Lemosina,
Via Turonensis; Via Tolosona, Via Podiensis.

II

Dorian, Phrygian, Lydian—
modes in diatonic sequence which would order
the response & antiphon at Cluny:

authentic, plagal; plagal and authentic—
hypodorian, hypomixolydian—
Magnificat! Magnificat anima mea Dominum.

And canticles in stone carved in capitals
to honor every mode
in which the honor of this Lady might

be chanted, melismatic even,
graced the choir itself in St. Hugh's hall
where someone wrote the book

sending walkers down the roads to Santiago.
Whose creation Aimery Picaud?
Whose persona Turpin? *The Codex Calixtinus!*

Book that wrought a miracle of power?
or book that answered it and echoed it, reflected
power trans-Pyrenean and uncanny,

causality determined by no human hand?
Did Santiago draw his pilgrims to his shrine,
or did the Monks of Cluny push?

Far from the basilica, far from
the *corona* with its hundred lamps & more lighted
there to brighten Pentecost or Easter, far

from the twelve arcades of double pillars,
the goldsmith's workshop & the bearded lutenist beside
the dancing girl celebrating in their frozen

artistry the artistry of monophonic provenance
which answered every gesture
of the vestured celebrant—and far, far before

the carving of a single capital,
the scribbling of a single line of Latin in a single book,
the hammering of gold, the glazing

of an ornament, the singing of the kyrie or gloria,
the censing of the host,
a strange boat arrived off Finisterre. . . .

(Or so they say. Or so they said
who made the book.) The boat came from Jerusalem
without a sail, without a rudder,

without oars. It bore his head beside his body
who had caught it when the sword
of Herod dropped it in his open hands.

It bore his two disciples. As they neared
the land beneath the *campus stellae*
where the lord of every geste would heave his

spear into the surf, drawn across the Pyrenees
by virtue of this other who would lie down now
for some eight hundred years—son of Zebedee

and Salomé, brother of St. John, son of Thunder
born into Galicia—
a bridegroom riding to his wedding reined

his horse in, stared a moment at the little boat,
galloped straight into the tranquil sea.
When horse and rider rose, both were covered with

the scallop shells that were his sign, his
awaiting Cluny and his cult
(the carving of the capitals, the canticles in stone,

the singing of the antiphons,
the scribbling of the Latin in his lenten book)
but also *hers*—

Magnificat! Magnificat anima mea Dominam—
who rose up on a scallop shell
to dazzle any bridegroom staring at whatever sea.

So it began. So they said it had begun.
A phase (a phrase (a moment in
the spin of some ephemeride (a change

not even in the modes of music
from the Greek
to the Gregorian. . . .

(And chiefly with an aim to rid the south of Moors, to rid it of the Mozarabic
taint in liturgies and chants, to blast the peasant heretics following the Gnostic light of
Avila's Priscillian. And then? Then the castigations of Bernard, the smashings of the
Huguenots, the marshals of Napoleon on the mountain trails, the slow dismantling of
the abbey for its stone, the twists of floral patterns on the broken columns standing in
the ruined granary, the Shell Oil station on the highway through the pass. And at the
restaurant by the river in St-Jean-Pied-de-Port (Michelin: 2 stars), good coquilles St.
Jacques . . .

III

Aimery Picaud to those who walked:
Beware the Gascons and beware the Basques:
drink only from this well, never

drink from that: these boatmen on that river
will deceive you: trust
only those who ply the other one: and if

you cross the mountains through
the path of Cize, he warned of Ostabat where men
appear with sticks to block your way

and then by force extract an unjust toll:
these men are fierce, the country they inhabit barbarous,
their tongue terrifies the hearts of all who hear:

God they call *Urcia,* bread is *orgui,* wine is *ardum:*
may the rich who profit from their tolls
and fares, the lords above the rivers & the king of Aragon,

Raymonde de Solis and Vivien d'Aigremont,
atone by long and public penitance; may any priest
who pardons them be smitten with anathema:

Depraved they are, perverse and lecherous,
destitute of any good; the men
and women show their private parts to pilgrims,

fornicate with beasts; the men kiss the vulva
of both wife and mule. When a man
comes in a house he whistles like a kite, & when

he lurks behind the rocks or trees
he hoots out like an owl or howls like a wolf:
Beware these Gascons & beware these Basques.

But at the gate of Cize rejoice!
From this high peak you gaze down at the western ocean,
at the frontiers of Castille & Aragon & France.

Here with axe and mattock, spade
and other tools Charlemagne's companions built a road
into Galicia: May their souls rest

in peace, and may the souls also of those others
who in times of Aldefonso & Calixtus
worked upon the road and made it safe rest in peace:

André, Roger, Avit, Fortus, Arnault,
Etienne and Pierre, who built the bridge again
over the Mino: for them, eternal peace.

If you cross the Somport pass
you come to several towns: to Borce first and
then to Canfranc, Jaca, Osturit,

Tiermas of the royal baths, and Monreal.
You will meet the road from Cize
at Puente-La-Reina. Estella has good bread,

good wine & meat & fish, and all things
there are plentiful. Past Estella flow the waters
of the Ega, sweet and pure, as are

these other rivers I now name: The Cea
by Sahagún, the Esla by Mansilla,
the Torio by León and near the Jewish camp.

If you come by Arles and Les Alischamps
you will see more tombs of marble
than you would believe carved in Latin dialect

spread before you more than one mile long
& one mile wide. If you come
by Arles you must seek the relics of

St. Honoratus and St. Gilles.
Between the branches of the Rhone, at Trinquetaille,
stands the marble column where the people

tied St. Honoratus and beheaded him.
He caught his head and threw it in the Rhone where
angels bore it to the sea and

on to Cartageña where it rests in glory
& performs great miracles.
Who would fail to kiss the altar of St. Gilles?

Who would fail to tell the story of his
pious life? On the golden coffer there behind his
altar in the second register are Aries,

Taurus, Gemini and Cancer with the other signs
winding among golden flowers on a vine.
A crystal trout stands erect there on his tail.

May the Hungarians blush to say they have
his body. May the monks of Chamalières be confounded.
I, Arnauld du Mont, transcribe today

the writings of Picaud, describe the roads the
states the castles towns and mountains
waters wells and fishes men and lands and saints

the habits customs routes and weathers in this
fifth book of the *Codex Calixtinus*
on the stages of the way to Santiago.

IV

From Mont Saint-Michel to Sens,
from Besançon to Finisterre, a darkness fell at noon,
the walls of houses cracked, down

from all the bell towers tumbled bells.
In the encampment, flames leapt from spears of ash & apple,
hauberks buckled, steel casques burst,

bears and leopards walked among the men in Charles' dream.
For so he dreamed. Dreamed within
a dream Roland's requiem before the ships

of Baligant sailed up the Ebro,
their mastheads and their prows decked and lighted
through the night with lamps and rubies

in the story that Turaldos tells.
(From Ostabat, the Port of Cize, Val Carlos—then
the high road trod by Gascons & the Basques:

The road below was made by strangers and their armies.
Turonensis, Lemosina, Podiensis:
Straight to Spain each one through Roncevaux.)

They came to him among the Saxons saying:
join us against the Omayyads
at Saragossa: march with us to Abd-al-Rahman's hall.

It was Suleiman himself, governor of Barcelona,
Abbasid and loyal to
the Caliphate of Baghdad. Charles made it a crusade.

Burgundians and Lombards, Goths and Provençals,
Austrasians and Bavarians
loyal to the Reich found themselves conscripted

for the Frankish Blitzkreig. For this was *Hereban:*
this was draft trumpeted by missi
all across Imperium: this was all incumbent on

vicarius and count. And so they came.
They came with sumpter, destrier,
& palfrey; they came with cooks & carpenters & sheep.

They marched away looking like a tribe of nomads
followed by the peddlers & the jugglers,
the singers & the whores. And crossed the mountains

at the Port of Cize. In the Cluny version
there is no Suleiman & no alliance.
Everything is supernatural power. The walls of Pamplona

fall at Charles' approach. He curses
and Luçerna is a great salt lake in which there swims
a single large black bass.

Turpini Historia Karoli: "I am James the son of
Zebedee whom Herod slew. My body
is Galicia. Seek me in this dream & I will be your stay.

My body is Galicia; my soul a field of stars."
Off he marched to Compostela;
At Finisterre he threw his spear into the sea.

In the lives of Einhard and The Stammerer, the facts;
In the *Geste* and *Codex,*
fear and hope and song:—

From Mont Saint-Michel to Sens,
from Besançon to Finisterre, a darkness fell at noon,
the walls of houses cracked, down

from all the bell towers tumbled bells.
In the encampment, flames leapt from spears of ash & apple,
hauberks buckled, steel casques burst,

bears and leopards walked among the men in Charles' dream.
For so he dreamed. Dreamed within
a dream Roland's requiem before the ships

of Baligant sailed up the Ebro,
their mastheads and their prows decked and lighted
through the night with lamps and rubies

in the story that Turaldos tells.
(From Ostabat, the Port of Cize, Val Carlos—then
the high road trod by Gascons & the Basques:

The road below was made by strangers and their armies.
Turonensis, Lemosina, Podiensis:
Straight to Spain each one through Roncevaux. . . .

Before the Codex made at Cluny, the Capitularies;
before the pseudo-Turpin, Turpin.
And afterwards the song. Afterwards the echoing of Roland's horn.

The nine hundred meters to the Vierge d'Orisson.
The planted crosses like a harbor full of masts.
Afterwards the E.T.A.,

the slogans of the separatists,
Afterwards the sabotaged refinery, the blown-up train.
Afterwards the dawn escape across the pass.

From Mont Saint-Michel to Sens,
from Besançon to Finisterre, a darkness fell at noon,
the walls of houses cracked, down

from all the bell towers tumbled bells.

V

Aoi.
Pax vobiscum, pax domini,
Aoi.
　　　Ainsi soit il.

And Charles murdered fourteen hundred Saxons
after Roncevaux, cutting off their heads,
when no one would reveal the hiding place of

Widukind, when no one would convert. A northern
paradigm for slaughters in the south?
At the far end of the trail, before there was a trail,

there were tales told: narratives of gnosis
whispered themselves north
to bleed in Roussillon when shepherds saw the

flocks of transmigrating souls walk among their
sheep looking for good company
and habitation. . . .
                              Even thus Galicia's Priscillian:

Executed 385 by Evodius, Prefect appointed
by the tyrant Maximus,
at the urging of Ithacius, his fellow Bishop. . . .

The soul, then, of its own will doth come to earth,
passing through the seven heavens, and
is sown in the body of this flesh. Or would one rather

say, as did Orosius to St. Augustine: "Worse than
the Manichees!" And the Saint: "Light!
which lies before the gaze of mortal eyes, not only

in those vessels where it shines in its purest state,
but also in admixture to be purified:
smoke & darkness, fire & water & wind . . . its own abode."

Along the Via Tolosona to Toulouse and then beyond
they told the tales: tunics of human flesh,
penitential wandering, sparks hereticated, vestures of decay.

They praised the seal of the mouth,
the seal of the belly and the hand; the demiurge
was author of this world;

among the rocks and trees, among the sheep
& cattle, they acknowledged each
the aeon that was only an apparent body, only born

apparently into the pitch and sulphur of a human shape
to utter human words. The words
they uttered and the tales they told were strange:

                    . . . when I was once
a horse, I lost my shoe between
the stones & carried on unshod the whole night long.

Cloven to the navel by this wound got of a Moor,
I speak to him alone who goes out
with the dead, the messenger of souls

who saw the lizard run into the ass's skull. . . .
The Ram presides above the head,
the Twins behind the loins. . . .
                              Were these voices then

an echo of a field of force counter to
the leys on which the houses of St. James aligned
themselves from north of Arles into Spain?

No Cluniac reform or Romanesque adornment to
the dogma from the rustic prentices of old Priscillian
dead eight hundred years before their time;

no chant in diatonic mode, in good Gregorian, but
diabolic danger here. This
called out for Inquisition and for blood.

Across all Occitania, across the Languedoc
and down the Via Tolosona spread
the news: Béziers was ruined and destroyed,

fifteen thousand fell before the walls & in the town
where mercenaries heard the knights cry out
to conjure holocaust: kill them all; God will know his own.

At Bram, Monfort gouged the eyes out, cut
the nose and upper lip off all survivors of his siege,
leaving just one man with just one eye

to lead his friends to Cabaret.
This was orthodox revenge. This was on the orders
of a man called Innocent.

Raymond of Toulouse, driven from his city,
fled to England, then returned
through Spain where troops passed down the Somport Pass

along the Tolosona to link up with his confederates,
the counts of Foix and of Comminges.
The chronicles explain that *everyone began*

to weep and rushed toward Raymond as he entered
through the vaulted gates to kiss
his clothes, his feet, his legs, his hands.

He appeared to them like one arisen from the dead.
At once the population of the town
began to mend the walls that Monfort had torn down.

Knights and burgers, boys and girls, great and small,
hewed and carried stones while troubadours
sang out their mockery of France, of Simon, of his son.

It was not enough. Though Simon died
outside the walls, the French king and Pope Honorious
concluded what the Monforts

and Pope Innocent began. Behind the conquerors
there came Inquisitors; with
the Inquisitors, denunciations, torture and betrayal.

But in the mountains and along the shepherds' paths
leading to and from the Tolosona trail,
the old tales nonetheless were whispered still

far from cities and the seneschals, far from
Bernard Gui, his book & his Dominicans.
The cycle of transhumance led itinerant *perfecti*

there among gavaches as far from their own ostals
as the Ariège is from Morella,
the wide Garonne from Ebro's northern bank & winter camp.

. . . tunics of human flesh,
penitential wandering, sparks hereticated, vestures
of decay. . . .

Among the rocks and trees, among the sheep
and cattle, they acknowledged each
the aeon that was only an apparent body, only born

apparently into the pitch & sulphur of a human shape
to utter human words.
And in Galicia, beneath the nave, restless with the centuries,

the east-facing tombs out of all alignment with
the Roman mausoleum & supporting walls
take up proximity below the bones in Santiago's vault

to something holy. The martyred heretic of Trier?
Aoi.
Pax vobiscum, pax domini.

      Aoi. Ainsi soit il.

VI

But was it this that found the floriations
in the columns, found in capitals
the dance that found the music of the cloister & the choir,

the song that found the south for Eleanor of Aquitaine?
Trobar, they said: to find.
To find one's way, one's path, to find the song,

to find the music for the song,
to find through stands of walnut, poplar, chestnut,
through meadows full of buttercups

and orchids, over or beside the banks of many rivers
from above Uzerche to well below
the Lot—Vézère, Corrèze, Couze, Dordogne, Vers—

along the paths of sandstone, rust red & pink,
the way through Limousin, through Perigord, all along
the Via Lemosina to a small road leading to

a castle gate, to find a woman in that place
who finds herself in song,
to find a friend, a fellow singer there or on the road.

Or to the north and west, at Poitiers,
along the Touronensis after
Orléans and Tours, to find before the heaths

of Gascony the pine forests and the *plat pays*
of Poitevins who speak the language
sung by William, Lord of Aquitaine, or the Lemosin

of singers who found comfort who found welcome
at his son's court, his who died
at Santiago, and the court of Eleanor his heir

whose lineage from Charlemagne found Angevin Bordeaux.
They came from Albi and Toulouse,
the town of Cahors and the county of Quercy,

but did they find for her and sing
the *Deus non fecit* of the heretic *perfecti* of Province
or the light from Eleusis

bathing trail and keep and column in its warmth?
Beneath the limestone cliffs of the Dordogne,
past the verges bright with honeysuckle, thyme and juniper,

quarried stone and timber floated toward the sea
on barges by the dark ores of the *causse,*
while salt, fish, and news of Angevin ambition & desire

came on inland from Bordeaux and from Libourne.
From Hautefort, Ribérek; from
nearby Ventadorn, singers found their way to Poitiers.

The sun rains, they sang: *lo soleils plovil,*
while pilgrims in Rocamadour
climbed toward what they sought, singing without benefit

of trobar ric or trobar clus: *midonz, midonz*
in a dazed vision of the lady there,
hunched & black upon a stick fallen from the sky.

To sing, to pray: to find behind them
south of Ventedorn, of Hautefort, of Cahors & Toulouse,
alignments in the temple of the sun

at Montségur measuring the solstice, measuring
the equinox, dawn light raining
through the eastern portholes of a ship

riding its great wave, counting down the year,
counting down the years, sign by sign
from Aries to The Fish, not to brighten only that

new morning in Provence but latterly to bend
also onto any path
of any who would follow, singing

at the gates of abbeys or below the castle walls
in any language found
where every song was fond

and yet forbidding, forensic as the night.
Did those who sang, do those who sing,
care at all that at the ending of their song,

as at the start, William of Aquitaine,
son of the troubadour, father of the child
they would hail in Poitiers

kneels crying *midonz* to the stars
but finds in Santiago's tomb not the bones of James
but those of the heretic Priscillian?

I am Arnaut who gathers the wind.
I am Arnaut who hunts the hare with the ox.
I am Arnaut who swims against the tide.

•

Near Excidieul, long long after Aquitaine
was France, after the end
of what was Angevin, and after the end of the end,

two lone walkers slogged along the road
and spoke of vortices
and things to be reborn

after Europe's latest conflagration. Was it spring? Was it 1920? The older of the
two, trying to remember after fifty years, could not be sure. It was he who had crept
over rafters, peering down at the Dronne, once before. He knew that Aubeterre was
to the east, that one could find three keeps outside Mareuil, a pleached arbour at
Chalais. He knew the roads in this place. He had walked into Perigord, had seen
Narbonne, Cahors, Chalus, and now was once again walking with his friend near
Excidieul. In certain ways he much resembled the old finders of song, and sang their
songs in his own way and tried to make them new. He called the other one, his friend,
Arnaut, though that was not his name, and stopped with him beside a castle wall. He
saw above them both, and wrote down in his book, *the wave pattern cut in the stone,
spire-top alevel the well curb,* and then heard this other say, the sun shining, the birds
singing, *I am afraid of the life after death.* Of a sudden. Out of the calm and clarity of
morning.

He stored the loved places in his memory—the roads, the keeps beside the rivers, the
arbour at Chalais—and walked in Eleusinian light and through the years to Rimini
and Rome, in darkness on to Pisa in another war. And after fifty years, and from the
silence of his great old age, he said: *Rucksacked, we walked from Excidieul. When he
told me what he feared, he paused, and then he added: "Now, at last, I have shocked
him. . . ."*

Who was Arnaut to gather the wind?

Intercalation

And who, asked the Doctor Mellifluus, were the Cluniacs to gather all *these* things: *deformis formositas ac formosa deformitas.* A wave pattern cut in the stone would have been enough—would have been, perhaps, too much. But apes and monstrous centaurs? half-men and fighting knights? hunters blowing horns? many bodies under just one head or many heads sprouting from a single body? Who were the Cluniacs to gather round them windy artisans to carve their curiosities, to carve chimeras, onto cloister capitals from St. Hugh's Hall to Santiago so that it became a joy to read the marbles and a plague to read the books. The concupiscence of eyes! For he had deemed as dung whatever shone with beauty. (Dung, too, was music and the talk, *humanus et jocundus,* of the monks, or the song of deeds in poetry. The concupiscence of ears! For he'd have silence, silence, save when he would speak, the great voice shaking his emaciated frame near to dissolution and yet echoing through all of Christendom: *Jihad! Jihad!* He looked upon the mind of Abelard, the body of Queen Eleanor, and did not like them. Man of the north, he gazed upon the south and built the rack on which they'd stretch the men of Langedoc after he'd made widows of the women standing horror-stricken outside Vézelay the day a thousand knights called out for crosses.) Contra Dionysius, the pseudo-Areopagite. Contra Saint-Denis. Contra Grosseteste, contra Bonaventure, and before their time. There was, he thundered, darkness in the light. And light in darkness of the fastness, of the desert, of the cave.

And yet, Abbot Suger sighed, thinking of his Solomon and walking in the hall the saint had called the Workshop of Vulcan, the Synagogue of Satan: *dilectio decoris domus Dei.* . . . *Cross of St. Eloy! Thy chrysolite, thy onyx and thy beryl.* It seemed to him he dwelt in some far region of the mind not entirely on this earth nor yet entirely in the purity of Heaven. . . . When he looked upon such stones. . . . When the sun's rays came flooding through the windows of the choir. For he was servant to the Pater Luminum and to the First Radiance, his son. Their emanations drenched so utterly this mortal world that, beholding them polluted even in the vestures of decay, we should rise—*animae*—by the manual guidance of material lights. The onyx that he contemplated was a light, the chrysolite a light, lights the screen of Charlemagne, the Coupe de Ptolemées, the crystal vase, the chalice of sardonyx, and the burnished ewer. Also every carving in the stones—the capitals, the portal of the west facade—and every stone itself, placed with cunning and with reverence according to the rules of proportion on the other stones, and then proportion too, laws invisible made visible by building—place and order, number, species, kind—these were lanterns shining round him which, he said, *me illuminant.*

But to Citeaux, but to Clairvaux: letters which began *Vestra Sublimitas* (and without irony). Acknowledging intemperance in dress, intemperance in food and drink; acknowledging the horses fit for kings and their expensive, sumptuous liveries; superfluities of every kind, excesses which endangered everything, opening the Royal Abbey to the winds of calumny. . . . He'd move into the smallest cell. He'd walk while others rode. He'd fast. . . . And yet expand the narthex and reconstruct the choir. Enlarge and amplify the nave. Find a quarry near Pontoise in which they'd cut no longer millstones for their livelihood but graceful columns by the grace of God. He'd execute mosaics on the tympanum, elaborate the crenellations. Hire castors for the objects to be bronzed, sculptors from the Cluniacs to carve in columns tall figures on the splayed jambs. Abolish compound piers and redesign triforia. Raise the towers up above the rose making of the rose itself a fulcrum. Repair the lion's tail that supported until recently the collonette. Repair zodiacal reliefs and, in the crypt, the capitals' eight abacus athemia. In the Valley of Chevreuse, he'd hunt himself for twelve tall trees, trunks sufficient in their height for roof-beams of his new west roof and fell them in the woods with his own axe, and offer thanks. Nor would he renounce the light—whatever letters went to Bernard of Clairvaux—the light proportionate unto itself, order mathematical of all diffusion, infinite in volume and activity, lux and lumen both.

And then at Vézelay, Bernard. Sunny Burgundy. The Via Podiensis and the city on the hill. Bishops, statesmen, peasants hungry for some kind of fair, thugs and mercenaries, Louis King of France who ached for glory and beside him Eleanor. Multitudes so many that they flooded all the fields waiting for the prophet from Clairvaux who would command them (Suger quiet under some far tree; Suger strong for peace). At Sens, he had destroyed Abélard. Now he'd widow all the women of the north. Rhetorician of the Holy War, demagogue of the crusade, he stood outside the abbey where the Pentecostal Christ of Gislebertus, *sol invictus* of the entry to the choir, measures time. But then what time was *this*, what year? Sea-green incorruptible beneath his Abbot's shroud, he numbered hours and souls in strict and occult symmetry. Were days measured once again by Kalends, Nones and Ides? Was solstice equinox and equinox the solstice? Did lunar phases intersect the solar year? Who had carved a column with the *lam* and *alif* of the Holy Name and was it *zenith* now or *nadir* in the Latin's Arabic? Many bodies sprouted from his head and many heads from every weaving body. Hautbois and bass bombarde began to play, shawm and chime and rebec as the voices sang *Fauvel* and *Reis Glorios*. From Mont Saint-Michel to Sens, from Besançon to Finisterre, a darkness fell at noon, the walls of houses cracked, down from all the bell towers tumbled bells. In a far encampment, flames leapt from spears of ash and apple, hauberks buckled, steel casques burst, bears and leopards walked among the men in Bernard's dream. For so he dreamed, even as he spoke. Dreamed within a dream Jerusalem's high requiem before the ships of Saladin sailed south from Tyre, their mastheads and their prows decked and lighted through the night with lamps and rubies in the story that the emirs tell. But everything would not be done at once. He saw emblazoned on a calendar suspended in the sky that it would be the year of Grace—but it would be no year of Grace when he awakened from his grave and found the month Brumaire: Those before him in the field walked straight over his indignant ghost and, shouting out obscenities, burned and looted in the abbey, then marched back down Via Podiensis and the Rue St. Jacques into the capital. All of Paris quaked beneath the church of St. Denis and night revealed itself in which the very stars went out as mobs broke in to take the challices, the vials, the little golden vessels used to serve the wine of the ineffable First Light, and swilled their brandy from those cups, then with clubs and hammers beat them flat. Long lines of priests in vestments led through burning streets a train of mules and of horses laden with patinas, chandeliers and censers from a dozen churches on the Santiago trail, pushed before them carts and wheel-barrows loaded with ciboriums and candle-sticks and silver suns. *Merde!* they shouted. *Vanities!* And tore from roofs and crannies sculpted figures wearing crowns to smash their eyes out and their jaws into a stony chorus of eternal silent screams. Relics torn from reliquaries fed the bonfires and the holy dead themselves were disinterred. Bells from Languedoc, from Conques, bells that rang above him there at Vézelay, were melted down for cannon and the cannon dragged along the trails into Spain to blast the columns and the capitals, the arms and legs and heads of kingdom come, into the brain of Goya—Vézelay's splayed Christ upon the door become the victims of the Tres de Mayo, the *deformis formositas ac formosa deformitas* of the twisted and uncanny *Disparates,* the black figures on El Sordo's Quinta walls.

. . . how many years?
The Abbot Suger did not know, but he was Regent.
He set about his work.

Pilgrims set off walking down the Via Podiensis from the church of Julien le Pauvre.

Part II: Spain

I

And from the ninety-second year of the Hegira
and from Damascus
and from the lips of Caliph Walid Abulabas:

permission for Tariq ibn-Ziyad to set forth
from Ceuta in his borrowed ships
to see if what was spoken by Tarif ibn-Malik

and his captives of al-Andalus
was true: serene skies, an excellence of weather,
abundant springs and many rivers,

fruit & flowers & perfume as fine as in Cathay,
mines full of precious metals, tall
standing idols of Ionians amidst extraordinary ruins,

and an infidel weak king despised by tribes & peoples
who but waited to be rendered tributary
to the Caliphate and subject to Koranic law.

And then: collapse of the Visigothic armies
at the battle near Sierra de Retín,
knights' bodies tossed into the rising Barbate

and the footmen with their slings & clubs & scythes
falling before Berber scimitars
days before the Qaysite and Yemeni horsemen

under Musa ibn-Nusayr could even cross
from Jabal Musa. Then the hurried crossing of the straight,
the meeting between Musa and Tariq at Talavera,

the occupation of León, Astorga, Saragossa,
and the messenger prostrate before the Caliph in Damascus
saying *Yes! Serene skies, an excellence of weather,*

abundant springs and many rivers, fruit and flowers
and perfume as fine as in Cathay,
mines full of precious metals and, inside this bag

I open for you now, O Caliph,
the severed head of Roderick, king of the Visigoths.
Behold the token of our victory!

Died al-Walid Abulabas in the ninety-sixth year
of the Hegira when, for his troubles,
Musa was condemned by Sulayman to prison & the bastinado

and Tariq ibn-Ziyad disappeared from every chronicle.
But the chronicles themselves go on:
A bad time for Umayyads at home, but every

kind of glory for the jihad in al-Andalus.
Which is why the hungry Umayyad, hunted in the streets
and alleys by the Abbasids, was going there:

the young man hiding in the rushes of Euphrates,
then a silhouetted horseman riding through the desert in the night,
the moon on his shoulder, the pole star in his eye.

Landing north of Málaga, he wrote his laws.
Having *crossed the desert*
& the sea & mastered both the wasteland & the waves,

he came into his kingdom, for he was Abd-al-Rahman
and would rule: *no one*
to be tortured, no one to be crucified or burned,

separated from his children or his wife, or anyone
to be despoiled of his holy objects
if in tribute come the golden dinars & the golden wheat

the flour & the barley heaped in bushels on the wagons
to be weighed, the measures
requisite of vinegar and honey, common musk & oil.

And Abd-al-Rahman rebuilt the mosque in Córdoba.
And the second Abd-al-Rahman
Gathered the philosophers and poets, gathered the musicians

and the concubines and wives. And the Sufi at the gates
called his heart a pasture for gazelles, said
he'd come to Córdoba following the camels of his love.

From the columns left by Rome there sprouted upwards
palm-like in oasis the supports
for Allah's double tier of arches, hemisphere

upon the square, fluted dome upon the vault. . . .
When they built the Alcázar &
Madinat al-Zahra, six thousand dressed stones

were called for every day, 11,000 loads of lime & sand.
There were 10,000 workmen, 12,000 mules.
By their kilns and pits, the potters & the tanners,

the armorers and smiths. . . . Plane, then, on plane . . .
the surface of each building there
a depth of arabesque, brick and faience overlaid

with geometric pattern & the forms of Kufic & Basmala
lettering interlaced with flowers,
framed by grape vine and acanthus all dissolving

strength & weight & structure in a dazzle of idea:
horror vacui: shifting ordering of order
all unseen, water of icosahedron, air of octahedron

fire of tetrahedron on the simple cube of earth,
living carpet in the grid of pathways behind walls,
sunken flower-beds, myrtle bushes

shading tributaries of the central pool and reflection
of the zones and axes of this world
crossing at the intersection where a Ziryab might play

his lute or al-Ghazal recite. . . . And Abd-al-Rahman
built on Abd-al-Rahman's work, &
Abd-al-Rahman brought it to completion. . . .

Who could have forseen in these expansive years
the squabbling of *taifas*
and Moorish rulers paying tribute to

Alfonso, Sancho, & Rodrigo Díaz El Campeador?
No one walked along the roads
to cross the Aragón where every route converged upon

a single bridge or sang the tales of El Cid & Charlemagne
slogging through Navarre into Castile.
But it was spring. Spring in Burgundy and spring

in all al-Andalus. In Cluny & in Córdoba they carved
stones and sewed the mint & the marjoram;
silkworms hatched & beans began to shoot and all

the apple & the cherry trees flowered white at once.
Water in the aqueducts was fresh as snow
in mountain streams, & everything it irrigated green.

But when the Sufi heard the flute notes in the air
and his disciple asked him
Master, what is that we hear outside the wall?

he looked up from the pile of sand on which he sat
reading the Koran and said:
It is the voice of someone crying for this world

because he wishes it to live beyond its end.
He cries for things that pass.
Only God remains. The music of the flute

Is the song of Satan crying in the desert
for the wells that all run dry,
for the temples & the castles & the caliphates that fall.

II

Via Tolosona, Via Podiensis.
There among the tall and narrow cypresses,
the white sarcophagi of Arles

worn by centuries of wind & sun,
where Charlemagne's lieutenants it was said
lay beside Servilius & Flavius

and coffins drifted down the Rhone
on narrow rafts to be unloaded by St. Victor's monks,
they walked: Via Tolosona.

Via Podiensis: They walked as well from
Burgundy through the Auvergne,
slogged along volcanic downland up into Aubrac

and on through Languedoc to Conques
and gazed into the yellow morning light falling
from above the central axis through

the abbey's lantern tower
and praised St. Foy, and praised as well
with Aimery Picaud their guide

the names of certain travelers
who had long before secured the safety of their way
and also other ways: Via Podiensis,

Via Lemosina, Via Turonensis.
They crossed the Loire at Tours and at Nevers,
walking toward Bordeaux or

from St. Leonard and St. Martial of Limoges
to Périgord and to Chalosse.
At Tours beside the sandy, wide & braided river

they would rest a while and bathe
or seek the narrow shoals nearby & shallow streams
that ran between. And read: *at the gate of Cize*

Rejoice! (Picaud, again Picaud) *And from this peak*
gaze at all the western ocean,
at the frontiers of Castille & Aragón & France.

Here with axe and mattock, spade
and other tools Charlemagne's companions built a road
into Galicia: May their souls rest

in peace, and may the souls also of those others
who in times of Aldefonso & Calixtus
worked upon the road and made it safe rest in peace . . .

For there were times when all was war.
There was a time, far into the south, when Muhammad's very arm
came to lie and work its magic

in the mosque at Córdoba, a time when Ibn Abi Amir
took it from its jewelled box
and shook it like a spear at Santiago,

made a Via Dolorosa out of every trail in Galicia
and lit a conflagration
which would burn beyond our cities & beyond his time . . .

From Mont Saint-Michel to Sens,
from Besançon to Finisterre, a darkness fell at noon,
walls of houses cracked, down

from all the bell towers tumbled bells.
In the encampment, flames leapt from spears of ash & apple
hauberks buckled, steel casques burst,

bears and leopards walked among the men in Picaud's dream.
For so he dreamed. Dreamed within
a dream Roland's requiem before the ships

of Baligant sailed up the Ebro,
their mastheads and their prows decked and lighted
through the night with lamps and rubies

in the story that Turaldos tells.
(From Ostabat, the Port of Cize, Val Carlos—then
the high road trod by Gascons & the Basques:

The road below was made by strangers and their armies.
Turonensis, Lemosina, Podiensis:
Straight to Spain each one through Roncevaux.)

And Almanzor al-Allah razed León
and burned the monasteries at Eslonza, Sahagún;
In Navarre, the king gave up his daughter;

counts became his vassals, one by one. On the road
to Córdoba weeping prisoners trod,
year on year from west of Saragossa. In Compostela,

he left not a stone. In Burgos not more than a promise:
That Almoravids would arise to follow him,
fakirs from the deserts of Sahara: that Yusuf ibn-Tashufin

would land in Algeciras, holy & appalling & austere.
His face entirely covered with a veil,
eating only bread and camel's flesh and honey,

he'd annihilate the armies of Alfonso at Sagrajas.
Widows and their children
would go begging on the ashen empty trails

and from Algeciras to the March,
from Marchlands to Finisterre, the dark would fall at noon,
the walls of houses crack, down

from all the bell towers tumble bells.

III

I commend my soul to God, and my remains,
If I be slain by Moors,
to Oña, to whose altar I bequeath

1,600 maravedis, three of my best horses,
two mules, my clothing with the
robes of ciclatoun & my three purple cloaks,

and also two silver goblets. If my vassals
do not bring my body back,
hold them in dishonor, treat them even

as the vassals who had murdered their own lord.
He was ransomed, Count Gonzalo Salvadorez,
and returning—but indeed to Oña to be buried there . . .

And Ramiro of Navarre was returning—
in an oaken coffin to the church of Saint Maria . . .
And the men of Logroño to Logroño,

the men of Pamplona to Pamplona . . .
and the open crypts at Jaca and Sangüesa and at Yesa,
the sepulchers of monasteries on the Ebro,

graves in the churchyards on the Oca and the Aragón,
all began to fill because again
Alfonso had not summoned Don Rodrigo from his exile.

Tañen las campanas en San Pero a clamor
por Castiella. . . . He has left Castile, the poet sang,
And they rang & pealed the bells,

but he had gone: at Bivar the gate was broken
on its hinges, the porch of his house was empty still;
there were no falcons there, & no molted hawks.

The portals of the city had been shut against him.
When he rode up to Burgos flying sixty pennons, he kicked against
the lock, shouted with the strength of sixty heroes

to the people of the city to admit him. But everybody
hid behind his curtained windows.
Alfonso had condemned Rodrigo Díaz, & because of this

Count Gonzalo Salvadorez and Ramiro of Navarre
had died in battle and the king's
beaten army was retreating from the castle at Rueda.

There was worse to come. At Sagrajas, in the south,
as had been foretold.
At Sagrajas, where they beat upon the drums all day.

At Sagrajas, by a tributary of the Guadiana
where Almoravids & the armies of al-Andalus allied themselves
but where Alfonso of Castile & León

failed again to summon Don Rodrigo Díaz from his exile.
Because of that, the Moor could write:
Do thou remember the times of Muhamad Almanzor,

and bring to thy memory those treaties where
thy fathers offered him the homage even of their daughters,
and sent those virgins for their tribute,

even to the far lands of our rule, even into Africa;
Bring this to thy memory before
presuming now to cast thunders against us,

before presuming now to menace us, for we have seen
you marching from the castle of Rueda with
the bodies of Gonzalo Salvadorez & Ramiro of Navarre.

But Alfonso would return the bells of Santiago
to Galicia, and he would boast: *I will*
redeem my word, I will preserve my plighted faith—

and fall upon thy lands with fire and sword
& drive you back into the sea.
There will be no further messages between us . . .

only the clangour of our arms, the neighing
of the war-horse, the blaring
trumpets and the thundering of atambours.

But riding south without Rodrigo Díaz, he would
soon be riding north—with bodies
of his knights and his confederates, knights & kings

to bury in their lands along the Ebro and the Oca and
the Aragón, where he was riding from Rueda
with the bodies of Gonzalo Salvadorez & Ramiro of Navarre.

Tañen las campanas en San Pero a clamor
por Castiella. . . . He has left Castile, the poet sang,
and they rang & pealed the bells,

but he had gone: at Bivar the gate was broken
on its hinges, the porch of his house was empty still;
there were no falcons there, & no molted hawks.

The portals of the city had been shut against him.
When he rode up to Burgos flying sixty pennons, he kicked against
the lock, shouted with the strength of sixty heroes

to the people of the city to admit him. But everybody
hid behind his curtained windows.
Alfonso had condemned Rodrigo Díaz, & because of this

Count Gonzalo Salvadorez and Ramiro of Navarre
had died in battle and the king's
beaten army was retreating from the castle at Rueda . . .

and because of this, the king would be routed
at Sagrajas by the Guadiana,
return with the bodies of his knights & his confederates

to bury near Gonzalo Salvadorez & Ramiro of Navarre.

IV

Oit varones una razón! he shouted
in the dusty square,
echoing the *Hoc Carmen Audite* of certain Joculatores,

Joculatores Domini, who stepped around him
and his eager rabble of an audience
to walk beneath the scaffold of the master of Sangüesa

who would freeze him there forever in the stone
even as he left the town
to sing the wayfarers upon their way

from Yesa on through Burgos to León.   ·
On the portal he disports himself with viol & bow,
and also with the lady in a sexy gown

whose other friend is farting in a well beside a cooper
struggling with his heavy barrel.
But on the trail he was quintessential news, was history itself,

and sang the life of Don Rodrigo while El Cid
yet earned the fame to warrant song.
And aged within his story. And grew so very old

his song became a banner among banners
of reconquest: *Oit varones*
una razón—of reconciliation on the Tagus, it might be,

once the hero halted at El Poyo,
once the heralds brought him followers from Aragón & Monreal,
once Minaya sought Alfonso for him

west in Sahagún, west in Carrión,
toward which they walked who'd gathered in the square
beneath the portal of María la Real.

And when Rodrigo rode to meet his king the villagers
& peasants saw, the singer sang
tanta buena arma, tanto buen cavallo corredor—

splendid weapons, swift horses, capes and cloaks
and furs and everyone
vestidos son de colores, all dressed in colors,

underneath the banners
when he stopped on the Tagus, when he fell upon
his face before Alfonso, when he

took between his teeth the grasses of the field—
las yerbas del campo—and wept
great tears as if he had received a mortal wound

and would be reconciled with the earth itself. . . .
as act of faith? Auto de fé?
& near the Tagus once again, Toledo's banners flying

long long beyond him who had come to meet Alfonso
from Valencia & him whose song
became a banner among banners of reconquest?

This *razón* was also sung along the trails, for it was news,
and it was news of conflagration
great as that which burned the northern cities

in the Caliphate: this *razón* was Torquemada's song.
Hoc Carmen Audite.
In conspecto tormentorum . . . (As when Don Rodrigo's daughters

lash and spurs were shown by their own bridegrooms.
When they entered the grove of Corpes
following the two Infantes back to Carrión near Sahagún.

. . . bien lo creades
aquí seredes escarnidas en estos fieros montes.
Oy nos partiremos . . .

And they knew it for a certainty that they
would be tormented
scourged and shamed and left in that dark place.)

Those abjuring marched with tapers through each town
& wore the sambenito & the yellow robe
embroidered with a black Saint Andrew's cross.

The crier walked before them, crying out
to those who came to watch
the nature of offenses to be punished while

behind them came the paste-board effigies
of those Marranos and Moriscos
who had died of torture, and exhumed bodies

of the heretics dead & buried before Torquemada
reigned at every quemadero:
Hoc Carmen Audite. In conspecto tormentorum. . . .

These we order vicars, rectors, chaplains, sacristans
to treat as excommunicated & accursed for
having now incurred the wrath & indignation of Almighty God

& on these rebels & these disobedient
be all the plagues and maledictions which befell upon
king Pharaoh and his host & may

the excommunication pass to all their progeny.
May they be accursed in eating
& in drinking, in waking and in sleeping,

in coming and in going. Accursed be they
in living & in dying & the devil
be at their right hand; may their days be few

and evil, may their substance pass to others,
may their children all be orphans & widows all their wives.
May usurers take all their goods;

May all their prayers be turned to maledictions;
accursed be their bread and wine,
their meat and fish, their fruit & any food they eat;

the houses they inhabit & the raiment that they wear.
Accursed be they unto Satan
and his lords, & these accompany them both night & day. . . .

But far from Toledo, on the road to Sahagún & Carrión,
they told the tales: tunics of human flesh,
penitential wandering, sparks hereticated, vestures of decay.

They praised the seal of the mouth,
the seal of the belly and the hand; the demiurge
was author of this world;

among the rocks and trees, among the sheep
& cattle, they acknowledged each
the aeon that was only an apparent body, only born

apparently into the pitch and sulphur of a human shape
to utter human words. And the Jews
hid their secret practices, and the Arabs likewise theirs,

and at the ending of the song, as at the very start,
Don Rodrigo asked his king,
earning thus his exile: *Did you kill your brother?*

Did you collude & commit incest with your sister?
For if you did, all your schemes will fail,
even though I lie prostrate before you eating grass. . . .

Take this oath upon the iron bolt, upon the crossbow.
Otherwise, may peasants murder you—
Villanos te maten, rey; villanos, que no hidalgos;

even though I lie prostrate before you eating grass. . . .

•

When the singer reached the bridge at Puente la Reina
with the pilgrims who had followed him
for some six hundred years, they met an army:

Soult and Ney & other marshals of Napoleon crossing
into Spain through Roncevaux
and trailing all the engines of their empire. . . .

. . . . *bien lo creades*
aquí seredes escarnidas en estos fieros montes.
Oy nos partiremos. . . .

Aoi.
Oit varones una razón.
Aoi.

Hoc Carmen Audite.

V

Soult was at Saldaña on the Carrión
when General Stewart's aide-de-camp walked into Rueda
past the cow-dung fires of peasants

to discover there some eighty horsemen who belonged,
he ascertained, to a division of
Franceski's cavalry. These the light dragoons surrounded

after midnight. General Moore advanced from Salamanca
through Alaejos to Valladolid, & a stolen
sabretache with full intelligence in Marshal Berthier's dispatch

revealed that Junot's infantry had yet to cross the Ebro
and that Ney was still engaged at Saragossa.
On forced march, the British trod December's icy roads

from Toro to Mayorga south of Sahagún.
What pilgrims they became!
Everyone a step-child to some devotee of Sol Invictus,

god of legionaries in whatever expeditionary war,
they billeted beneath the frieze
of Saint María del Camino with its bulls' heads

on abutments of the inner arch, racing horsemen,
and a naked rider on a lion.
They'd drag like Mithra in a week their burdens

down unholy trails and over mountains to the cave
that was Coruña. Exactly where the spears
of Charlemagne's unburied dead had sprouted leaves

along the Cea at the edge of Sahagún, they halted
their advance. By Alfonso's grave,
by the graves of Doña Berta & Constanza, his French queens,

by the ruins of the abbey that had rivaled Cluny
built by Jaca's Englishman
where Aimery Picaud had found unrivalled natural beauty

and a city radiant with grace,
these Englishmen of Sir John Moore's found news:
that Bonaparte himself had crossed the Duoro

and would crush them where they were or drive them
to the sea. They turned and fled;
joined a procession of the living and the dead.

Before them, taurophorus, Mithra dragged the bull,
took its hooves upon his shoulders,
pulling it up mountain trails after Villafranca

in the sleet and snow. Behind them, in his death,
embalmed Rodrigo—tied to beams
that braced him in his saddle, dressed for combat,

sword in hand, looking like some exhumed agent
of the Holy Office driving
heretics to new trans-Cantabrian quemaderos. . . .

. . . *tantas lancas premer e alçar,*
tanta adágara foradar e passar. . . . tanta loriga
falssar e desmanchar, tantos pendones

salir vermejos en sangre. . . . lances, bucklers,
coats of mail broken there,
pennons of the foreign legions soaked in blood . . .

If Suero de Quiñones read aloud the twenty-two
conditions of the tournament
in which he'd win his ransom at the Orbiego bridge

and then proclaim the Paso Honroso,
who would answer for these blood-shod infantry between
Bembibre and the Cua not *Oit Varones* . . .

but *Ahora sueña la razón?*
If reason dreamt on this retreat, then so did song.
It slept and dreamed its monsters

in the language of a soldiery that spat and swore
cursing all the bridges
that would measure honor & had measured piety before.

No one shouted *Vivan los Ingleses* as they passed
through villages to loot & rape
where church bells rang when they had gone to summon Soult.

Stragglers broke into bodegas, smashed the wine casks,
then cut up the dying mules & bullocks
by the roadside that had pulled artillery & ammunition vans

to boil them in kettles on great fires they built with gun butts
and mix with what remained of issue brandy,
salted meats and biscuits and the buckets full of melted snow.

Those who dared to sleep were frozen dead by morning,
and when chasseurs came in twos & threes
to scout the strength of Moore's rear guard, they hacked

the arms off those who staggered in the wind
or split their heads down to their chins with sabers flashing
in the sun. All the rest was in the hills.

From Villafranca to Nogales, from
Nogales on through Lugo to Betanzos, darkness fell at noon,
the walls of houses cracked, down

from all the bell towers tumbled bells.
On the march, flames leapt from spears of ash & apple,
hauberks buckled, steel casques burst,

bears and leopards walked among the men
in John Moore's dream. For so he dreamed. Dreamed
within a dream his own high requiem before

the English ships sailed north from Vigo,
their mastheads and their prows decked and lighted
through the night with lamps and rubies

in the story that Trafalgar tells.
Miles, Corax, Heliodromus, Pater of the bas-reliefs,
he signed the zodiac of Mithra's solstice

and hallucinated Corybantes in the skins of beasts
and flagellants where General Paget
sought to make example of deserters and had lashed

at stunted icy trees men who'd
hidden in the windowless dark huts with sick & filthy
mountaineers and who, blinded by the days

of snow, could only hear what would accompany
their punishment: a jangling
of the manacles and fetters hanging on the branded

criminals who crawled the road before them
on their hands and knees and slept
with lepers under dark façades of abbeys, while

in Bonaparte's Madrid, El Sordo painted bulls.
Bulls and bodies of the slain—
dismembered and hung up on trees like ornaments:

arms and legs, heads with genitals stuffed
in their mouths, torsos
cut off at the waist and neck and shoulders.

These the *deformis formositas ac formosa deformitas*
of the hour—torsos and toros,
packed in ice, delivered down the trails to Picasso

in a year when internationals once more decamp in Spain. . . .
Viva la Muerte's the Falangist song.
Lorca's murdered; Machado & Vallejo promptly die.

Trusting neither Mithra nor St. James, his eye
on anarchists in Barcelona,
Franco summons mercenary Moors to save the church.

VI

In the high places, they could hear the blast.
Ships rocked on the sea,
the houses at Coruña shook on their foundations

when the ammunition stores were blown.
At Santiago, bells that had burned Almanzor's oils
rang from the shock of it while men

whose job it was to ring them stood
amazed out in the square & wondered if this thunder
and the ringing was in time for Vespers

or for Nones or if it was entirely out of time.
The thunder and the ringing echoed
down the trails, back to San Millán, San Juan de la Peña,

while Maragatos looked up from their plows
and Basque shepherds among flocks near Roncevaux
turned their backs on the west & hunched

down under tall protective rocks jutting up
in frosty and transhumant fields.
Then in the high & highest places everything was still.

As it was in the beginning. Before Saint Francis
came down from the hills to Rocaforte,
before he taught his brothers how to preach & sing the word

to their little sister birds who flew into the tallest trees
and over cliffs in threefold
colored and adoring coats; before the Logos

or the Duende moved in Bertsulari singing ancient
fueros of the Basques; before Ignatius
hammered out his disciplines among the mountain rocks

breaking on the igneous of will the *ignis fatuus*
of valleys & the vagaries of love.
As it was in the beginning. . . .

                         Long before *it is*
and ever shall be under overhanging
rocks at San Juan de la Peña . . . where they say, they *say*

the Grail came to rest and made a fortress
of the monastery there carved beneath a cliff-face roof
where dowsers conjured water out of rock

in Mithra's Visigothic cave & his tauroctonous priest
drove the killing sword, like Manolete,
in the shoulder of the bellowing great beast

to burst its heart & bleed the plants & herbs across
the mountainside that monks would one day
gather there, bleed the wheat they'd make into their bread.

Everything, everything was still. As it was in the beginning
long before the silence of the abbeys,
the silence of the abbots in their solitary prayer,

the silence of the brothers cutting hay & tending sheep
at San Millán of the Cowl,
the silent sacristan measuring and pouring oils—

the weavers and the tailors and the copyists at work,
Cellarius among his stores of wool and flax,
Hortulanus in his garden tending bees—silence broken only

as Hebdomadarius, finished with the cooking, rings a bell
and even old Gonzalo de Berceo looks up happily
from silent pages where his saint has walked the mountains

in the language of Castillian *juglares* which is not,
God knows, the language of the Latin clerks. *Andaba por los montes,*
por los fuertes lugares, por las cuestas enhiestas,

but silently, and all around him it was very very still.
As it was in the beginning before silence,
in the silence that preceded silence, in the stillness

before anything was still, when nothing
made a single sound and singularity was only nothing's
song unsinging . . . aphonia

before a whisper or a breath, aphasia
before injury,
aphelion of outcry without sun . . .

                                    Long before *it is*
and ever shall be under overhanging
rocks at San Juan de la Peña, at San Millán of the Cowl,

at Loyola's Casa-Torre and the shepherds' huts
of Bertsulari in the Pyrenees
when no one spoke of *fueros* or *tristitia* or *spes,*

and there were neither rights nor hopes nor
sadnesses to speak of.
Then in the high and highest places everything was still.

As it was in the beginning. As it will be in the end.

         •

Towards Pamplona, long long after all Navarre
was Spain, and after the end
of the Kingdom of Aragón, & after the end of the end,

I, John, walked with my wife Diana
down from the Somport Pass following the silence
that invited and received my song

after Europe's latest referendum. In the city of the *encierro* and the festival of
San Fermín, we drank red wines of the Ribera—Baja Montaña, Tierra Estella—
hosted by Delgado-Gomez, genius of that place and guide Picaud. From university to
citadel to bull ring, from cathedral to the Plaza del Castillo and along the high banks
of the Arga, we walked and talked about the road to Santiago, El Cid Campeador,
Zumalacárregui and Carlist wars. For he, Delgado-Gomez, was a native of that
place. He knew the way to San Juan de la Peña, to Leyre and Olite and Sanguessa—
and so we followed him along the river valleys, into hills, and over arid plains in the
Bardenas. And after seven days and seven nights remembering the likes of Sancho the
Wise and Sancho the Strong, the battle of Navas de Tolosa and the chains of Mira-
mamolín wrapped around a coat of arms, the three of us, blest and besotted, burned

by the sun but refreshed by all the waters of the mountain streams, the shade of many cloisters, and the breezes of the vineyards of Mañeru, crossed the Puente la Reina ourselves, and walked that trail leading to the sea at Finisterre.

And, in the high & highest places, everything was still.

Afterword and Notes

Because these poems span three decades, I need to say a few words about them in order to establish some contexts. I also feel compelled to express some ambivalence about the first two pieces, *Poem in Three Parts* and *Bucyrus*.

Shortly after I wrote *Bucyrus,* I read W. H. Auden's Foreword to the 1966 Faber and Faber reprint of *The Orators*. "As a rule," Auden said, "when I re-read something I wrote when I was younger, I can think myself back into the frame of mind in which I wrote it. *The Orators,* though, defeats me. My name on the title-page seems a pseudonym for someone else, someone talented but near the border of sanity, who might well, in a year or two, become a Nazi." I had two feelings when I read this. The first was a kind of incredulity—certainly Auden was being disingenuous about not being able to remember the frame of mind he was in when he wrote his book—and the second was a kind of predictable young man's annoyance that the older Auden felt a predictable compulsion to disown his early work. Still a few years closer to *Poem in Three Parts* and *Bucyrus* than Auden was to *The Orators* when he wrote his Foreword, I now find myself more than half inclined to disown them. And yet, like Auden with his *Orators* in 1966, I am in fact re-publishing the pieces. If *I* want to disown these poems (and I think of *Bucyrus* as a poem rather than as a story), *he*—the young poet still buried somewhere inside me in the same way that I was once buried inside him—wants to claim them proudly. "What energy!" he says. Auden must have heard a similar voice saying much the same to him.

Unlike Auden with respect to *The Orators,* I do remember pretty clearly the frame of mind I was in when I wrote these pieces and, I think, the major historical factors that conditioned them. *Bucyrus* was written in California in 1966 during the period of anti-war protests, LSD taking, The Beatles and the Rolling Stones, Ken Kesey in the hills above Stanford University and Allen Ginsberg in San Francisco. *Poem in Three Parts* was written in the *Annus Mirabilis* itself, 1968, in the same summer that Peter Michelson, to whom the poem was dedicated, drove with me to Chicago to join the protests at the Democratic national convention and experience the police riot prepared for all of us by Mayor Daley. But neither *Bucyrus* nor *Poem in Three Parts* is actually about the 1960s. History conditioned these poems, but not by providing them with a contemporary subject matter in the manner of certain sonnets in Robert Lowell's *Notebook* or Norman Mailer's *Armies of the Night*. History goaded them to be—goaded me to make them—almost gratuitously violent. That is what troubles me about them.

The literary influences on *Poem in Three Parts* are easy to recognize. The third part is pure Charles Olson; the first and second are Robert Duncan spliced with early Kenneth Rexroth spliced with Peter Michelson's *Pacific Plainsong* (which was being written down the road from me in South Bend, Indiana during the same summer). In the background hovers a later and permanent influence on my work: David Jones. In spite of the pastiche, what still makes the poem feel authentic after all these years is the music of several of its sections and the way it settles into an engagement with aspects of my family's history which are still important to me. It is more difficult to locate models for *Bucyrus*, but I do remember having read just before its composition quite a lot of Gertrude Stein.

The original notes still serve fairly adequately as an account of the scholarly sources for these poems. L. Ron Hubbard, an obscure quack in 1966, became eventually a famous quack. (My own brush with Dienetics and the Scientologists occurred early—straight out of high school at the University of Utah in 1959.) It amuses me that Hubbard keeps such easy company in this piece with the likes of Richard Baxter, Julio Caro Baroja, Jules Michelet and Margaret Murray. It is worth blaming the distinguished Medievalist, V. A. Kolve, for the alchemy. Had he not assigned me to research the alchemical backgrounds of Chaucer's *The Canon's Yeoman's Tale* at Stanford University in 1965, I might never have read Carl Jung or any of the others on this fascinating and disturbing subject. As for witchcraft, that is part of the permanent history of the west. I wish I could give adequate acknowledgement to Derek Wavell, whoever he may be. All the quotes from Chuang Tze (misspelled "Chuang Tz" in the original printing of the notes) came from a story of his called *The Belinda File* in a long defunct Cambridge literary magazine the title of which I cannot remember. I have never read Chuang Tze.

The *Stefan Batory* and *Mihail Lermontov* poems would seem to be made from the antimatter of *Poem in Three Parts;* they belong as much to the Seventies as the earlier poem does to the Sixties. The first was written on the Polish liner Stefan Batory while travelling to America during the last stages of the Watergate controversy after a year in England. The second was written two years later on a Russian ship, the Mihail Lermontov, as I returned to England to spend a year at Cambridge. Both poems aim at comedy in the broadest sense, not satire. The cold war, of course, was still on; no one could have predicted then what was going to happen in 1989. Originally dedicated to my daughters, the full title of the first printing read: "The Stefan Batory and Mihail Lermontov Poems—Being, among other things, a comic lament for the decade of the 1960s, and a private celebration, both early and late, of the American Bicentennial and the Queen's Silver Jubilee." The attempt to locate a matrilineal descent for myself in the Lermontov cycle is, in spite of all the joking around, perfectly serious. I hope too that it makes up for—or at any rate balances—the masculine violence of some sections of *Poem in Three Parts.*

Northern Summer was begun in Fife, Scotland, on the Wemyss Castle estate in the summer of 1980 and finished three years later in the Cambridgeshire village of Trumpington. It was written at a time when my family and I had lost our summer home in Suffolk, the place where I had done most of my writing for fifteen years and more. The attempt to integrate myself with this particular landscape and history was not, it seems to me, successful; and the poem deals with an ultimately alienating experience. Perhaps for this reason, the most important section is the seventh, "A Voice," where in fact I hear not only my mother's voice reading from Stevenson and Scott, but also my wife's reading the same texts to our daughters.

At this point, it will be enough to reprint the original notes on sources for *Poem in Three Parts, Bucyrus, Batory, Lermontov,* and *Northern Summer,* together with the notes for *An East Anglian Diptych, Facts from an Apocryphal Midwest,* and *A Compostela Diptych* as they originally appeared in *A Gathering of Ways* (1991).

Bucyrus & Poem in Three Parts

Bucyrus makes use of several short quotes each from James W. Bright's *Anglo-Saxon Reader* and Richard Baxter's *The Saints' Everlasting Rest,* as well as certain statements attributed to L. Ron Hubbard in an article on Scientology published in *Life* magazine at some point in the middle-to-late 1950s. Part One of *Poem in Three Parts* takes testimony and narrative from Margaret A. Murray's *The Witch-Cult in Western Europe,* narrative and commentary from Jules Michelet's *Satanism and Witchcraft* and from Kurt Seligmann's *The History of Magic,* and occasional details from Jean Lhermitte's *True and False Possession.* The concluding prose paragraph is from United Press International. Although the formulae in Part Two of *Poem in Three Parts* come from a number of primary sources (Paracelsus, Basil Valentine, Roger Bacon, Petrus Bonus, Albertus Magnus, Cornelius Agrippa, Norton, Asmole, Ripley, etc.) my immediate source was usually John Read's *Prelude to Chemistry.* For interpretation I have drawn most heavily on Jung's "The Idea of Redemption in Alchemy" from *The Integration of the Personality,* Frederic Spiegleberg's *Alchemy as a Way of Salvation* and my own *Th' Entencioun and Speche of Philosophers* (unpublished). The prose paragraph beginning "Whether the canons were ever intended to be sung . . ." is from F. H. Sawyer's "The Music in 'Atlanta Fugiens,'" printed as an appendix in Read. Part Three of *Poem in Three Parts* gets its law from Henry L. Stevens, Jr., Presiding Judge in the Superior Court of Carteret County, North Carolina, 1944: *Mrs. Alice Hoffman and Bogue Banks, Incorporated vs. Llewellyn Phillips and John Marshall Matthias, Trustee, The Alden Corporation and R. N. Larrimer.* It gets its philosophy from Chuang Tze out of Derek Wavell's *Belinda File,* and some of its incidents and details from an article by Robert Sullivan in the *Sunday News* (Oct. 7, 1945) and from accounts given me over the years by my parents—who were there. Other writings from which I have profitted in a general way during the composition of these collages include: Emile Durkheim, *The Elementary Forms of the Religious Life;* Paul Christian, *The History and Practice of Magic;* John Middleton, ed., *Magic, Witchcraft, and Curing;* Jacobus Sprenger and Heinrich Kramer, *Malleus Maleficarum;* Max Marwick, ed., *Witchcraft and Sorcery;* Pennethorne Hughes, *Witchcraft;* A. E. Waite, ed., *The Hermetic Museum* and *The Hermetic and Alchemical Writings of Paracelsus;* M. Caron and S. Hutin, *The Alchemists.*

The Stefan Batory Poems and The Mihail Lermontov Poems

Batory: Adam Mickiewicz, *Pan Tadeusz* (in the G. R. Noyes translation); *Adam Mickiewicz* (Unesco Books: essays by several hands); V. L. Benes and N. J. G. Pounds, *Poland;*

Tadeusz Ocioszynski, *Poland on the Baltic;* Jerzy Jan Lerski, *A Polish Chapter in Jacksonian America;* Henry Beston, *The St. Lawrence;* Guilbert Parker and Claude G. Bryan, *Old Quebec;* Eric Zagrans, two rejected lines from an early draft of his translation into Yiddish of "The Love Song of J. Alfred Prufrock." **Lermontov:** *The Poetry of Lermontov* (edited and translated by C. E. l'Ami); *A Lermontov Reader* (edited and translated by Guy Daniels); Mihail Lermontov, *A Hero of Our Time* (in the Nabokov translation); Janko Lavrin, *Lermontov;* Serge Sovietov, *Mickiewicz in Russia;* Edward J. Brown, *Russian Literature Since the Revolution;* Yon Barna, *Eisenstein;* Colette Shulman, ed., *We the Russians;* James H. Billington, *The Icon and the Axe;* Robert Payne, *The Fortress;* Charles M. Wiltse, *The New Nation;* R. C. McGrane, *The Panic of 1837;* N. K. Risjord, *The Old Republicans;* Sir Edward Creasy, *15 Decisive Battles;* Alan Wykes, *An Eye on the Thames;* Basil E. Cracknell, *Portrait of London River;* Philip Howard, *London's River;* A. P. Herbert, *The Thames.*

Northern Summer

Sir William Fraser, *Memorials of the Family of Wemyss of Wemyss;* Goran Sonnevi, "Void which falls out of void . . ."; *The Gododdin;* Antonia Fraser, *Mary Queen of Scots;* Robert Gore-Browne, *Lord Bothwell and Mary Queen of Scots;* Moray McLaren, *Bonnie Prince Charlie;* John Prebble, *Culloden;* Sir Wilter Scott, *Waverley;* Robert Louis Stevenson, *Kidnapped;* Jenni Calder, *Robert Louis Stevenson;* A. N. Wilson, *The Laird of Abbotsford;* Adam Smith, *The Wealth of Nations;* Fred R. Glahe, *Adam Smith and the Wealth of Nations;* R. B. Haldane, *Adam Smith;* E. W. Hirst, *Adam Smith;* John Rae, *The Life of Adam Smith;* John Fleming, *Robert Adam and His Circle;* James Macpherson, *The Poems of Ossian;* Derick S. Thomson, *The Gaelic Sources of MacPherson's Ossian;* Bailey Saunders, *Life and Letters of James Macpherson;* Henry Mackenzie, *The Man of Feeling;* Gerard A. Baker, *Henry Mackenzie.*

An East Anglian Diptych

This is very much a "poem of place" located in those parts of Cambridgeshire, Suffolk and Norfolk linked by the ley lines and rivers which connect locality with locality, and time with time. The ley lines in question are the ancient paths and tracks which date back to the neolithic period. The chief ley line followed is the Icknield Way, the track explored by Edward Thomas in his final volume of prose on the English countryside. Thomas himself figures in the prose section of the first part of the sequence, section iv. The controlling myth for both "Ley Lines" and "Rivers" derives from T. C. Lethbridge's *Gogmagog: The Buried Gods,* which treats the old Celtic/Belgic religion in terms of his excavation of the Wandelbury chalk figures and their relationship to better known hill figures such as the

Cerne Giant. The presiding presences in "Ley Lines" (who also return in "Rivers") are the dowser—Lethbridge himself was a dowser) and his prototype, the Dodman, who was the prehistoric surveyor who aligned the paths and tracks. The transition between the "Ley Lines" section and the "Rivers" is made by way of the terrestrial zodiac at Bury St. Edmund's, a vast arrangement of figures by means of which I move from the Sagittarius beginning on the River Lark near Abbots Bridge in Bury to the Gemini (in the form of Wandil, the East Anglian devil) standing on the Stour near Clare Castle. The rivers dealt with are, in order, the Stour, the Alde, and the Deben. As in "Ley Lines," this section shuttles backwards and forwards in time, though its geographical or topological movement is direct enough. This part too has a section in prose, John Constable on the Stour corresponding to Edward Thomas on the Icknield Way. The gods and goddesses invoked in both sections are the same: Gog (the sun/Bel/Baal/Belenus/Helith, etc.), Magog (the moon/Meg/Magg/Epona, etc.), and Wandil (darkness/the East Anglian devil/the giant with a sword, etc.). When the last section of "Ley Lines" moves into the present by counting off the numbers which locate Whittlesford church on the Ordnance Survey Map, the fit of alliteration is not gratuitous. The Shiela-na-gig figure over the Whittlesford church door is an image of Gogmagog, and Lethbridge argues that words like "goggle," "giggle," "ogle," and the child's grotesque toy "Golliwog" are all verbal derivations. The end of "Rivers," like the end of "Ley Lines," also moves into the present—but without the fit of alliteration.

Sources: T. C. Lethbridge, *GogMagog;* Shirley Toulson, *East Anglia: Walking the Ley Lines and Ancient Tracks;* W. G. Arnott, *Alde Estuary, Orwell Estuary: The Story of Ipswich River, Suffolk Estuary: The Story of the River Deben;* George Ewart Evans, *The Pattern Under the Plough, Ask the Fellows Who Cut the Hay;* Julia Pipe, *Port on the Alde;* R. Allen Brown, *Orford Castle;* F. J. E. Raby and P. K. Baille Reynolds, *Framlingham Castle;* O. R. Sitwell, *Framlingham Guide;* Julian Tennyson, *Suffolk Scene;* Rupert Bruce-Mitford, *The Sutton Hoo Ship Burial;* Bernice Grohskopf, *The Treasure of Sutton Hoo;* Michael Alexander, trans., *Beowulf;* W. J. Ashley, ed., *Edward III and His Wars, 1327–1360;* Michael Prestwich, *The Three Edwards;* William Longman, *The Life and Times of Edward the Third.*

Facts from an Apocryphal Midwest

I have grappled in this poem with some midwestern American geography, geology, prehistory and history that parallel in many ways those I was working with in "An East Anglian Diptych." The chief trails this time—American ley lines, as it were—began as prehistoric paths down which Lake Superior copper was carried from the early days of the Mound Builders until the collapse of their particular economy and way of life. These trails, and especially the Old Sauk Trail and the St. Joseph-Kankakee portage, were later used by the Potawatomi, the Miami and other local Algonquian tribes, as well as by the Iroquois on their raids into the area, and by the French explorers, traders and missionaries. Again, as in the East Anglian poem, three rivers figure in the topographical configuration that emerges: the St. Joseph (which the French called the River of Miamis), the Kankakee (also called the Seignelay), and the Illinois. The dominant historical figure in the poem is Réné-Robert Cavelier, Sieur de La Salle. Having begun my research while still at work on "An East Anglian Diptych" and having determined to write about rivers and trails which I often crossed but as yet knew little about, I found myself stimulated by exactly those things which from time to time I had thought might stimulate "another poet" as I sat writing about things I knew and loved in East Anglia—La Salle's voyage through the great lakes and journey along the local paths and waterways, Algonquian (mostly Potawatomi) history and mythology, the geological and geographical transformations which occurred during the last glacial recession, and the prose of Francis Parkman in the volume of *France and England in North America* called *La Salle and the Discovery of the Great West.* What had begun as an act of will rapidly became, in the actual processes of composition, altogether something else. Although I do not take La Salle all the way to the Mississippi (usually called the Colbert in the poem), I take him pretty far down the Illinois. For some of the same reasons that Edward Thomas and John Constable appear in "An East Anglian Diptych," Parkman himself appears briefly here. His prose is sometimes quoted, paraphrased, versified. Where quotations are not exact, I intend no disrespect. Formal constraints now and then demanded slight modifications in rhythm, diction and syntax. Neither Fenimore Cooper's stagecoach ride into the area nor the dedication of the cornerstone of the La Salle Memorial Project are fictions. The merging of the two, however, in the context of a pageant which occurred at the quatro-millennial anniversary of the La Salle-Miami Council is only a convenient way, consistent with the conclusions of both "Ley Lines" and "Rivers" in "An East Anglian Diptych," to bring the poem into the present historical period.

Among the sources for this poem are three that very few readers will have come across. These are books by an almost vanished breed, the local amateur historian. Charles H. Bartlett's *La Salle in the Valley of the St. Joseph,* George A. Baker's *The St. Joseph-Kankakee Portage,* and Timothy Edward Howard's *A History of St. Joseph County* were all enormously useful. Other sources for the poem include: Charles Haight Farnham, *A Life of Francis Parkman;* Howard Doughty, *Francis Parkman;* Louise Phelps Kellogg, *Early Narratives of the Northwest* and *The French Regime in Wisconsin and the Northwest;* Henri Joutel, *A Journal of La Salle's Last Voyage;* Carl O. Sauer, *Seventeenth Century North America* and *Selected Essays 1963-1975;* James A. Clifton, *The Prairie People;* R. David Edmunds, *The Potawatomis;* George T. Hunt, *The Wars of the Iroquois;* Fay Folsom Nichols, *The Kankakee;* Archer Butler Hulbert, *Indian Thoroughfares;* Hugh Brody, *Maps and Dreams;* Andrew Trout, *Jean-Baptiste Colbert;* James Fenimore Cooper, *The Oak Openings: or The Bee Hunter;* George Dekker, *James Fenimore Cooper: The American Scott;* Blake Nevius, *Cooper's Landscapes: An Essay on the Picturesque Vision.* The dedication of this poem reflects formal debts as well as friendship. "An East Anglian Diptych" began as a homage to David Jones and Robert Duncan. The present poem, beginning with its title, takes a leaf from Ken Smith's *The Poet Reclining* and some strategies from Michael Anania's *The Color of Dust* and *Riversongs.*

A Compostela Diptych

The final poem in what, from the summer of 1984 to the winter of 1990, slowly took the form of a trilogy, deals with the most distinguished trails of them all: the pilgrimage routes to Santiago de Compostela. Having written two poems where I felt on very familiar ground —though in two different ways—I began in 1986 to meditate a poem about a ground with which I was totally unfamiliar, except through the literature to which it had given birth from the troubadours to Walter Starkie and Eleanor Munro. In the summer of 1987 I walked parts of the Via Tolosana over Somport Pass and on through Jaca, San Juan de la Peña, Leyre, Sanguesa, Pamplona, Puente la Reina, Estella, Logroño, Nájera, Santo Domingo de la Calzada, and Burgos, crossing back into France through the pass at Roncesvalles. I did not reach Santiago itself, and I do not reach Santiago in the poem. The writing, however, became a pilgrimage in earnest when, without warning, I had first to help another person struggle towards physical and spiritual health, and then, unwell myself, begin a similar journey of my own.

As with the two earlier poems in the trilogy, I have more debts than I can possibly acknowledge. Stylistically, David Jones is once again a welcome and benevolent presence. Indeed his good help and hope have actually become, in a sense, one of the subjects of the present poem. The same could be said of Ezra Pound up through the walk from Excidieul. I have leaned heavily on a number of translations. Although the poet knows the various languages which he must sometimes quote all too imperfectly himself, the poem's polylingual texture is essential: it is necessary for the reader to try and hear the Latin, French, Spanish and Provençal words as best he can. I need particularly to acknowledge W. S. Merwin's translation of the *Poema del Cid*, Robert Harrison's and Dorothy L. Sayers' translations of the *Chanson de Roland*, and the three translations, one into French and two into English, of the Pilgrim's Guide attributed to Aimery Picaud from the *Codex Calixtinus* listed below with my full range of sources. Walter Starkie's *The Road to Santiago*, Roman Menéndez Pidal's *The Cid and His Spain*, and Eleanor Munro's *On Glory Roads* have been my constant companions. (Much in Part I derives from Munro's interpretation of the visual setting and internal structures of pilgrimage in the light of archaeo- and ethno-astronomical theory.) Occasional phrases from these books turn up in the poem itself, as also from the texts by Meyer Shapiro, Erwin Panofsky, Umberto Eco, Jules Michelet, Thomas Carlyle, Desmond Seward, Jacques Lacarriere, Emmanuel Le Roy Ladurie, Henry Chadwick, Alphonsus M. Liguori, Edward Peters, John James, Jan Read, J. A. Condé, Oleg Grabar, Henry Kamen, Christopher Hibbert, Franz Cumont, Henry Sedgwick, Johan Huizinga, Bruno S. James, Edgar Holt and Adam Nicholson listed below. Borrowings in the poem are usually indicated by italics.

Sources for Part I: Jeanne Vielliard, *Guide De Pèlerin de Saint-Jacques de Compostelle* (Texte Latin du XIIe Siècle, Édité et Traduit en Francais d'Après Les Manuscrits de Compostelle et de Ripoll); Constantine Christofides, *Notes Toward a History of Medieval and Renaissance Art, with a Translation of 'The Pilgrim's Guide to Saint-James of Compostela';* Paula L. Gerson, Annie Shaver-Crandall, & M. Alison Stones, eds. & translators, *Pilgrims' Guide to Santiago de Compostela;* A. Kingsley Porter, *Romanesque Sculpture of the Pilgrimage Roads;* Meyer Sharpiro, *Romanesque Art;* Joseph Gantner, *The Glory of Romanesque Art;* Vera Hell, *The Great Pilgrimage of the Middle Ages;* Eusebio Goicoechea Arrondo, *The Way to Santiago; El Camino de Santiago: Guia Del Peregrino;* Eleanor Munro, *On Glory Roads: A Pilgrim's Book about Pilgrimage;* Walter Starkie, *The Road to Santiago;* Noreen Hunt, *Cluniac Monasticism in the Central Middle Ages, Cluny Under Saint Hugh 1049–1109;* Jacobus de Voragine, *The Golden Legend* (translated and adapted from the Latin by Granger Ryan and Helmut Ripperger); Christopher Page, *Voices and Instruments of the Middle Ages: Instrumental Practice and Songs in France 1100–1300;* Russell Chamberlin, *The Emperor Charlemagne;* Charles Edward Russell, *Charlemagne: First of the Moderns;* Peter Munz, *Life in the Age of Charlemagne;* H. R. Loyn and John Percival, *The Reign of Charlemagne: Documents on Carolingian Government and Administration;* H. W. Garrod and R. B. Mowat, eds., *Einhard's Life of Charlemagne;* Robert Harrison, trans., *The Song of Roland;* Dorothy L. Sayers, trans., *The Song of Roland;* Edward Peters, *Heresy and Authority in Medieval Europe;* Msgr. Leon Cristiani, *Heresies and Heretics;* St. Alphonsus M. Liguori, *The History of Heresies, and their refutation* (trans. from the Italian by the Rev. John T. Mullock); Henry Chadwick, *Priscillian of Avila;* Jacques Lacarriere, *The Gnostics;* Emmanuel Le Roy Ladurie, *Montaillou: The Promised Land of Error;* Joseph R. Strayer, *The Albigensian Crusades;* Desmond Seward, *Eleanor of Aquitaine: The Mother Queen;* Johan Huizinga, *The Waning of the Middle Ages;* Peter Makin, *Provence and Pound;* Adam Nicholson, *Long Walks in France.* Sources for "Intercalation": Erwin Panofsky, ed. and trans., *Abbot Suger on the Abbey Church of St.-Denis and Its Art Treasures;* Umberto Eco, *Art and Beauty in the Middle Ages;* Bruno S. James, *Saint Bernard of Clairvaux;* Donald Francis Firebaugh, *St. Bernard's Preaching of the Second Crusade;* Thomas Merton, *The Last of the Fathers;* Henry Adams, *Mont-Saint-Michel and Chartres;* Steven Runciman, *A History of the Crusades;* Odo of Deuil, *De Profectione Ludovici VII in Orientem;* John Hugh Hill and Laurita Lyttleton Hill, *Raymond IV Count of Toulouse;* Jules Michelet, *History of the French Revolution,* Vol. VII (Books 14, 15, 16 and 17), trans. by Keith Botsford; Thomas Carlyle, *The French Revolution;* John James, *The Traveller's Key to Medieval France: A Guide to the Sacred Architecture of Medieval France.* Sources for Part II: J. A. Condé, *History of the Dominion of the Arabs in Spain;* Jan Read, *The Moors in Spain and Portugal;* Oleg Grabar, *The Formation of Islamic Art;* Keith Albarn, Jenny Miall Smith, Stanford Steele, Diana Walker, *The Language of Pattern;* W. S. Merwin, trans., *The Poem of the Cid* (with facing page Spanish text of the edition of Ramon Menéndez Pidal), *From the Spanish Morning: Translations of Spanish Ballads;* Ramon Menéndez Pidal, *The Cid and His Spain, Poesia Juglaresca y Origenes de las Literaturas Romancias;* Ernest Merimée and S. Griswold Morley, *A History of Spanish Literature;* David William Foster, *The Early Spanish Ballad;* Cecil Roth, *The Spanish Inquisition;* Henry Kamen, *The Spanish Inquisition;* David Gates, *The Spanish Ulcer: A History of the Peninsular War;* Richard Humble, *Napoleon's Peninsular Marshals;* Christopher Hibbert, *Corunna;* W. H. Fitchett, ed., *Wellington's Men: Some Soldier Autobiographies;* C. S. Forester, *The Gun;* Hugh Thomas, *The Spanish Civil War;* Franz Cumont, *The Mysteries of Mithra;* M. J. Vermaseren, *Mithras: The Secret God;* Francisco Goya, *The Complete Etchings,*

Aquatints and Lithographs; Eleanor Elsner, *The Romance of the Basque Country and the Pyrenees;* Johannes Jorgensen, *St. Francis of Assisi;* Omer Englebert, *Saint Francis of Assisi;* Henry Dwight Sedgwick, *Ignatius Loyola;* Mary Purcell, *The First Jesuit;* Walter Nigg, *Warriors of God: The Great Religious Orders and their Founders;* W. S. Porter, *Early Spanish Monasticism;* Edgar Holt, *The Carlist Wars in Spain.*

A Note about the Author

A native of Ohio, John Matthias teaches English at the University of Notre Dame. He has been Visiting Fellow in Poetry at Clare Hall, Cambridge, and lived for much of the 1970s in the East Anglia region of England. He has published five previous volumes of poetry with Swallow Press: *Bucyrus* (1971), *Turns* (1975), *Crossing* (1979), *Northern Summer: New and Selected Poems* (1984), and *A Gathering of Ways* (1991). *Bathory & Lermontov* (1980) and *Två Dikter* (1989) were published in Sweden. With Göran Printz-Påhlson, he edited and translated *Contemporary Swedish Poetry* (Swallow, 1980) and with Vladeta Vučković he translated *The Battle of Kosovo* (Swallow, 1987). His own work has been translated into Swedish, Dutch, French, German, Greek, and Serbo-Croat. He has edited *23 Modern British Poets* (Swallow, 1971), *Introducing David Jones* (Faber and Faber, 1980), and *David Jones: Man and Poet* (The National Poetry Foundation, 1989). His literary essays are collected in *Reading Old Friends* (SUNY Press, 1992). Simultaneously with *Beltane at Aphelion,* Swallow Press is publishing *Swimming at Midnight: Selected Shorter Poems.*